Otherworldly Affaires

Other books by Brad Steiger published by Anomalist Books:

Shadow World
Worlds Before Our Own
Strange Guests

Otherworldly Affaires:

*Haunted Lovers,
Phantom Spouses,
and Sexual Molesters
from the Shadow World*

Brad Steiger

Anomalist Books
San Antonio * New York

CONTENTS

1. APPARITIONS SEEN OF LOVED ONES AT THEIR MOMENT OF DEATH

Mrs. Stanley Waddell had not really expected to sleep well on that August night in 1948. Her husband lay in a coma in General Hospital and his doctor had informed her that the end was near.

"There's nothing more that you can do here," the physician had advised her. "Why don't you leave the hospital and get some rest?"

Mrs. Waddell had explained to the doctor that she felt that her place must be at her husband's bedside. "What if he should awaken and not find me there?" she had asked. "And it is too far to drive home only to come back if he needs me."

"Your husband has not been conscious for days," the doctor had said. "You appear to be on the brink of exhaustion. What good can you be to your children if you end up sick and in the hospital yourself? Get a room in a hotel near the hospital. Let the front desk know your number as soon as you've registered. I promise to call you if there is any change in your husband's condition."

Mrs. Waddell had caught a glimpse of herself in a large corridor window that the night's blackness had given a mirrorlike property. Her red-rimmed eyes looked deep-set because of the dark circles beneath them. Her hair was unkempt, disarrayed. Her face was puffy from crying, wan from lack of sleep. Perhaps the doctor was right, she had decided. She had better get some rest.

Now she lay beneath crisp hotel sheets, hoping that the drone of the air-conditioner might lull her to sleep. She checked her watch for what must have been the twentieth time since she had lain down shortly after midnight. It was 3:47 A.M.

Then, strangely, Mrs. Waddell sensed a familiar presence. "Stanley," she whispered, as she turned over on her back and sat up in bed.

She could see her husband clearly in the dim light of the hotel room. Somehow, in a manner that she would never be able to understand, Stanley stood at her bedside.

"I am leaving you now," Stanley said, his voice full and rich, as it had been before the terrible illness had wasted his strength, his body, even the timbre of his speech. "This old shell I've been using is no longer of any value to me. Don't worry. I'll always watch over you and our baby daughter."

Mrs. Waddell sat motionless long after the image of her husband had faded from the room. She was convinced that Stanley was dead, that his spirit had actually come to bid her good-bye, but grief had not been able to penetrate the dazed mental condition in which the sudden appearance of the apparition had left her. The part of her brain that was still thinking, still functioning, kept expecting the hospital to call and inform her of Stanley's death.

The call did not come until 10:00 A.M., more than six hours after her husband's apparition had appeared to her.

After she had attended to some of the details at the hospital, Mrs. Waddell asked to see her husband's ward doctor. When the physician asked politely if there were something that he might do for her, she asked if she could see her husband's chart.

"That's highly irregular and against hospital rules," the

doctor began, then, struck by something in Mrs. Waddell's manner, ceased his mechanical recitation of hospital dogma. "Why do you wish to see your husband's chart, Mrs. Waddell?"

"I would very much like to verify the precise moment of my husband's death," she explained. "I . . . I have a strong conviction that Stanley died at 3:47 A.M., even though the hospital did not phone me until 10:00 A.M. Please, doctor," she said softly. "It is very important to me to know this."

The physician called to a nurse seated at a desk to bring Stanley Waddell's chart. When he had it in his hand, his eyebrows raised, and he showed the chart to Mrs. Waddell, his forefinger pointing to the time of death—3:47 A.M.

Mrs. Waddell's eyes brimmed with tears. She had not been dreaming. Stanley had appeared to her. Her beloved husband had come to bid her good-bye and to offer her dramatic evidence of the human personality's ability to survive the death experience.

As she turned to leave the ward, the nurse touched Mrs. Waddell gently on the arm. "You knew, didn't you? Somehow you knew the exact moment your husband's soul left his body."

Mrs. Waddell nodded, unable to speak in her deep emotion.

"Someday," the nurse said, "I pray that I might experience proof of the soul's survival after death."

This chapter shall concern itself with accounts of men and women whose dying loved ones seem to have given them dramatic evidence of the soul's continued existence after the physical death of the body. Documented stories of such apparitions may be found in the literature of all eras and all cultures. Images of loved ones who have come to say farewell, to offer comfort and solace before their transition to another plane of existence, appear to rich and poor alike.

The question of whether or not such images actually appear to surviving loved ones has no revelancy to those men and women who have witnessed the apparition of a dear mate or sweetheart at the moment of their death or to those researchers who have spent many years of serious inquiry into the matter. As Andrew Lang once wrote: "Only one thing is certain about apparitions, namely, they do appear. They are really perceived."

The question which may remain is whether the percipients actually observed a discarnate entity, which occupied an objective area in time and space, or whether they perceived the result of a successfully implanted telepathic message-image, which had been transmitted at the moment of death by the dying loved one.

Whether the percipients whom we are about to meet were truly visited by the discarnate personalities of their loved ones or whether they but received a last telepathic message which became externalized by their own minds, we cannot dismiss their experiences as only dramatic devices of their imaginations. In each of the cases which we shall examine, the apparitions left the percipient with some bit of veridical information, information which was previously unknown to the percipient and which could be later verified (*e.g.*, Mrs. Waddell learning that the apparition of her husband appeared to her at the actual time of his death).

This would seem to be the place to distinguish the various differences between the disparate phenomena known as apparitions and ghosts.

A ghost appears at the same place at regular intervals, like a bit of motion-picture film which keeps being replayed whenever someone of the proper telepathic affinity sets the psychic "projector" into operation. A ghost seldom conveys any information to the percipient; indeed, a ghost rarely notices or interacts with a percipient in any way. Perhaps a ghost may best be defined as an animated memory pattern somehow attached to a place wherein a scene of strong emotion may have occurred.

An apparition, on the other hand, is always known and identified by the percipient. An apparition seldom appears more than once, and nearly always delivers information which is immediately intelligible and personally meaningful to the percipient.

Whether such apparitions represent a last cry of love from the innermost spirit or the actual discarnate spirit come to bid a loved one *au revoir,* the accounts which follow gave inestimable solace to the surviving lovers.

Mrs. Gerald Blanchard used to tease her husband that their love would have to last forever, because her wedding ring was so tight that she would never be able to get it off her finger. "And that's the way it'll stay until I tell you differently," Jerry would always reply with a chuckle.

There were few things to laugh and to tease about in 1944, especially if one were the wife of a serviceman. In November of that year, Jerry Blanchard was shipped overseas to the European theater of action, and his wife decided to live with his parents on their old farm homestead in New England. The Blanchards treated their daughter-in-law with warmth and consideration, and they gave her Jerry's old room, complete with its own stone fireplace. Each night at dusk Mrs. Blanchard would build a roaring fire on the grate, and in the morning she would revive the cherry-red coals with fresh fuel.

The progress of the war in Europe dominated nearly every dinnertime conversation, and by mid-January, 1945, things were going badly for the Allies. The Nazis seemed to sense that they had lost the war and they were determined to make the Allies pay dearly for their victory. A letter from Jerry arrived, and she read it aloud to his parents. Although censorship requirements would not allow him to be specific, Jerry wrote in general terms about preparations for a major offensive.

Two nights after she had received the letter from her husband, Mrs. Blanchard remembers going to sleep filled with prayerful concern for Jerry's safety. "I prayed for an awfully long time," she recalls; "then I fell asleep watching the flames swirl up the stone chimney."

She awakened sometime that night, her entire being suffused with terrible cold. "I felt cold and clammy clear to the bone. I sat up in bed to see if the fire had gone out, and I saw Jerry standing there. His features were clearly distinguishable in the red glow of the fireplace, and he looked tired and sad. He just stared at me for the longest time; then he leaned over and gently slipped my wedding ring off my finger. I'll never forget how cold his hands felt. He opened his mouth as if he were going to speak to me; then he disappeared."

Mrs. Blanchard blinked her eyes in disbelief and looked about her room, seeking reassurance of reality from its familiar fixtures. The fire in the grate was very low. It would soon be morning. She pulled the heavy quilts over her shivering frame and lay in silence until she heard the morning sounds of the Blanchard family shaking off sleep. When she was certain that everyone was up and assembled in the kitchen for breakfast, she came out to tell the family of her strange dream of Jerry.

"That was no dream," Jerry's grandmother said, shaking her head wisely. "Our poor Jerry is dead."

Mrs. Blanchard protested. It had only been a dream, nothing more.

"Then where is your wedding ring?" Grandmother wanted to know. "Where is that ring that none of us have ever seen you remove?"

Mrs. Blanchard clutched her hands together as if she could somehow prevent the ring's escape. She looked at her ring finger for the first time since she had awakened, and she was startled to see that it no longer bore the wedding band that had so tightly encircled it.

They found her wedding ring on the dresser, and Mrs. Blanchard could offer no explanation of how the snug band had been removed from her finger. Grandmother insisted that the explanation had already been told: the spirit of Jerry had removed it when he had come to say good-bye.

Two weeks later a telegram arrived from the War De-partment informing them of Jerry Blanchard's death in military action. He had been killed on February 8. The image of Jerry had appeared to his wife shortly after that, on February 9.

The above case is made all the more interesting because of the apparition's physical action of removing the tight ring from the woman's finger and transporting it to the dresser. One might argue, of course, that Mrs. Blanchard, upon receiving a telepathic impression of her dying hus-band, externalized an apparition of him and removed the ring herself in a kind of somnambulistic trance state. But to insist that the whole matter belongs in the realm of coin-cidence seems to constitute an argument woefully lacking in substance, an argument satisfactory only to the most devout skeptic. The fact that Mrs. Blanchard had such a dream of her husband removing her wedding band, thus symbolizing the termination of their earthly bond, on the very day of his death in a land thousands of miles away, seems most definitely to suggest a strong telepathic link-up between dying husband and anxious wife.

Jane Davies and Victor Mayer had been sweethearts since their puppy-love days back in elementary school. Jane's parents were transferred to another city when she and Victor were juniors in high school, and the two young people were heartbroken at the thought of a separation of several hundred miles. At first they talked of running away together and getting married, but common sense prevailed. They would write each other religiously and visit one an-other during every holiday. They would plan to attend the same college upon graduation from high school, where they would then be able to continue their romance as more mature young people.

One night after the teen-agers had been separated for

about two months, Victor looked up from his homework, distracted by what he thought must be a wisp of smoke drifting toward him. He had lain down on his bed after dinner with his social-studies book in his hands. Mom's good cooking and the extra laps at track that afternoon had begun to take their toll of his ability to concentrate. He had just been drifting off to sleep when he was snapped back to full awareness by strange tendrils of smoke moving toward him.

His first thought was that there might be a fire in the house, but he could not smell anything burning. He knew that he should get up to investigate, but he felt strangely apathetic, almost immobile. He was content to lie still and watch the mysterious smoke swirl about in the air.

Within a few moments the smoke had congealed into a cloud; then the cloud began to take on the figure of a woman. Soon features were discernible, and Victor was shocked to recognize his beloved sweetheart, Jane.

"I could not believe my eyes," he wrote later. "I rubbed at my face with my palms and ground my fists in my eyes. I had to make sure that I was not dreaming or that I had not fainted. I got off my bed and started toward the cloudy thing that had become Janie. Before I could touch it, however, it gave me a sad smile and disappeared. I was completely dumbfounded. I sat back on my bed, feeling like all the blood had been drained from my body."

Victor had acquired the habit of keeping a daily journal in which he recorded all significant personal experiences. When he had regained his emotional control, he went to his desk and recorded the date and the hour at which he had perceived the apparition. Two days later, Victor's parents received word that Jane Davies and her older sister had been killed when the car in which they had been riding had stalled on the tracks at a railroad crossing as the driver tried to beat the engine. The time of Jane Davies' death corresponded exactly to the time that Victor had recorded the appearance of the apparition.

The alert reader has noticed that the percipients in the three cases just presented have had one important physical condition in common: each of them perceived the apparition of a loved one while in bed—either just awakening from or just drifting into sleep. As one investigates accounts of such apparitions, and, indeed, many other manifestations of paranormal phenomena, one is struck with the realization of what fertile psychic ground lies in the hypnagogic state, that nebulous somewhere between waking and sleeping. Many researchers have theorized that it is while the percipient of the paranormal is in this psychic "twilight zone" that his unconscious is able to free itself from the inhibiting influence of the conscious and become more aware and more in tune with the various mental impressions which may be vying for attention.

In the following account, however, both percipient and witness were wide awake.

"My mother had been terribly lonely for many years after Dad died," writes Loretta Cochran. "I could not help being very pleased when she married Martin Crown, a widower who had suffered much heartache in the years since his wife and three daughters had been killed in an airplane crash."

At the time of the manifestation, Miss Cochran was seventeen, still living at home with her mother. She recalls that her mother and Mr. Crown had enjoyed several months of happiness when his business called him to another state.

"I was getting ready for a date," Miss Cochran recalls, "when we heard a knock at the door. Since I had not yet finished applying my makeup, I asked Mom to answer the door. I was a bit chagrined at my date for coming so early, but Mom smiled and told me to be happy my young man didn't just sit out in his car and honk for me.

"I was seated before my bedroom mirror, hastily applying eye shadow. I heard Mom open the door, and I could hear her mumbling, but I couldn't understand what she was saying. I couldn't figure out why she didn't ask my date to come in. I got kind of upset, thinking maybe he was telling her that he couldn't go out that night. But that didn't make sense. Why would he have come over to tell me such bad news when he could have telephoned?

"In a few seconds, Mom entered my room. She looked pale, and she was chewing at a corner of her lip in a way she does when she is nervous. 'That was Martin,' she said in a puzzled tone.

"She sat quietly on my bed for a few moments before she spoke again. We both knew that Martin had been gone for about a week, and we did not expect him to return home for at least another week. 'When I asked him to come into the apartment,' Mom continued, 'he just stood there, shook his head sadly, and turned away from me.' "

Miss Cochran ran to the front door of their apartment and opened it. Martin Crown was nowhere to be seen. She ran quickly down the stairs. There was no car in front of the apartment house, and she could see no men walking on the street. He could not have disappeared from sight in the few seconds which had passed since the two women had heard the knock at the door and the brief time in which Miss Cochran's mother had told her that Martin had appeared at their door.

"Just as I was about to return to our apartment," Miss Cochran writes, "my date arrived. I asked him if he minded if we stayed with my mother for just a few minutes before we left. I could guess what was going through Mom's mind, and I didn't want her to be alone just then. When we entered the apartment, Mom was on the telephone. When she hung up, she nearly became hysterical. Martin's business partner had called her to say that Martin had just been stricken with a heart attack and had died at the very moment that his ghost had knocked on our door."

In the account reported by Miss Cochran, it is interesting to note that the phenomenon of the apparition was objective enough so that both she and her mother heard the knock at the door. Although the younger woman did not see the image of her mother's husband, she was aware that the older woman was carrying on a conversation with someone at the door who refused to enter the apartment. In her girlish chagrin, she assumed that it must be her date with an excuse not to go out that night. Instead, it was the apparition of a sorrowful lover who had come to inform his new mate that the season of their flowering love was to be a tragically short one. ·

William E. Sorensen claims to have discovered an account of an apparition that appeared to the dying man's affianced sweetheart, together with five witnesses. According to Sorensen, who told his story in the July, 1959, issue of *Fate* magazine, he discovered the tale written on yellowed sheets in an old Bible which belongs to a cousin who lives in Holstedbro in Jutland, Denmark.

Eighteen-year-old Dora Starcke, who later became Dora Sorensen, the grandmother of William and his cousin, was engaged to marry Arne Borglum, a cavalryman who was among the first men called in 1864 when Denmark was attacked by Germany and Austria. Dora and Arne planned to be married as soon as he could manage a long furlough, but in the meantime, the young warrior had to be with his troop at the border.

Shortly after 8:00 P.M. on April 18, 1864, Dora, her parents, her two brothers, and her sister were seated in the parlor of the farmhouse. The family was occupied with reading, knitting, and casual discussions of planting time.

"Suddenly," writes Sorensen, "they saw Arne standing just inside the door leading to a hall. He looked exactly as when they last had seen him, except that he was pale, his blue uniform was splotched with mud, and his saber was missing—the scabbard at his side hung empty."

Mr. Starcke particularly noted the empty scabbard, for

he had been a cavalryman himself. The entire family sat before the image of Arne Borglum in complete bewilderment. The last they had heard, he was stationed at the front. Slowly they rose and started toward him to welcome him. They would learn how he had arrived and how he had managed to enter the house so quietly just as soon as they had shaken his hand.

Dora could imagine only one thing. Arne had been granted the long furlough for their wedding, and she ran to embrace her fiancé. She was within but a few feet of Arne when he vanished forever from her sight.

Since the apparition had been so clearly seen by all six members of the Starcke family, their reaction was one of "consternation and grief." According to Sorensen, the Starckes "held no doubt regarding the ominous significance of the vision."

About a week later, a letter from one of Arne Borglum's comrades told how Arne had died in fierce combat on a road near Flensburg. Arne had singlehandedly fought off five Austrian hussars, but one of them managed at last to shoot him in the back and to wrest the saber from his dying hand. Arne had died at the precise time that his apparition had appeared at the Starcke farmhouse. The image of Arne Borglum had manifested itself to his fiancée and her family exactly as he had appeared at the moment of his death, even to the empty scabbard at his side.

An account reached this author not long ago which told of how a man received what was to him convincing subjective proof that the human personality survives the death experience.

Charles Flandre had left the bedside of his wife, Laura, who was dying of leukemia. The ordeal had been a long and painful one for his poor wife, as well as having been an expensive and exhausting one for Mr. Flandre. "Please go home and get some rest," Mrs. Flandre said. "You must not stay here another night worrying over me. Go home and see to the children."

Flandre told his wife that he would go home, look in on the children and her mother, who had come to help with baby-sitting and the housework, but that he would come back to the hospital to be at her side. Laura only smiled.

"I saw that the children were all right and that Laura's mother had already gone to bed," Flandre recalled. "I checked my watch, then decided that I would nap for just a few minutes before I returned to the hospital.

"I couldn't have been sleeping more than twenty minutes when I felt what I knew to be the touch of my wife's lips on my cheek. It was a kiss of sweetness and love, a kiss that only Laura could have given me. No one will ever be able to convince me that it was not my wife who kissed me at that moment.

"I opened my eyes and sat up. I had left a small lamp on in the room before I had lain down to rest. I knew that someone else was in that room. Then, in a darkened corner, I caught a movement out of the corner of my eye. I turned to see a figure that seemed to be formed from a million tiny, sparkling stars. Although I could distinguish no features, the figure had a human-like shape. It seemed to raise its arms and float up out of sight through the ceiling.

"When I called the hospital a few moments later, I was not surprised to learn that Laura had just died. The night nurse had just been about to call me. She spoke a few words to console me, but I had just received the greatest kind of consolation from my Laura, who had come to prove to me that there is life beyond physical death."

Although Mrs. Harvey Stentor knew that her father had hardening of the arteries and often became mentally confused, she had long been annoyed by the fact that he had referred to her mother as "that old lady" when she had died.

The Harbots had been for a walk in the small park above

their home when Mrs. Harbot had suffered a sudden stroke and had fallen to the sidewalk. Mr. Harbot had been leaning on his cane with one hand and resting his arm on Mrs. Harbot when she had made a gasping sound and collapsed. Mr. Harbot had also been carried to the ground by the force of her fall, and the two elderly people had been found pitifully intertwined. Mrs. Harbot had died without regaining consciousness, and Mr. Harbot had been brought home to the residence of his daughter, Mrs. Stentor, seemingly more confused than ever.

"Esther was dying and leaving me," he told Mrs. Stentor. "I wanted to talk with her longer, but that old lady knocked into me and we both fell to the sidewalk. How I wish that she hadn't knocked me down."

Mrs. Stentor wrote: "I had been so shattered by the loss of my mother that it was difficult to be patient with Dad. He seemed to be concerned only that Mother had knocked him down when she had died. And it offended me that he kept referring to her as 'that old lady.' "

Mrs. Stentor resolved to be as compassionate as possible, and for several months she simply "tuned out" whatever her father had to say about her mother's death. Then one day he said something that made her listen to his mumblings with interest. "I wonder," Mr. Harbot mused into space, "if that old lady died, too?"

"What do you mean when you wonder if *she* died, *too?*" Mrs. Stentor asked. "Tell me again how Mother died."

"We were walking in the park, like we always loved to do," Mr. Harbot began. "Then Esther stopped me, and said that she was sorry, but that it was time for her to go . . . to die. I begged her not to leave me, but she left my side and began to walk down the hill toward the pond where the swans swim. A golden shaft of light came down from the sky, and two tall men in flowing robes stepped forward to take Esther by the hand. I called to her again, and she turned as if to tell me good-bye. But I never heard what she said, because that was when that old lady stumbled against me and knocked me down."

In her account of the experience, Mrs. Stentor wrote that for the first time she realized that her father had not associated Esther, her mother, with the "old lady" who had pulled him down with her to the sidewalk. Upon further questioning, Mrs. Stentor learned that, in his mental confusion, her father had seen his wife as she had appeared when she was much younger. The apparition that had come to tell him farewell was an image of his Esther in the full bloom of her womanhood, not the wrinkled "old lady" who had knocked him down at such an inopportune moment.

The case of Mr. Harbot seems to argue for the theory that the apparition is the result of a successfully implanted telepathic message which becomes externalized by the percipient's own mind. The confused mental processes of the elderly Mr. Harbot perceived his Esther as she once was, not as she existed at the moment of her death. If the apparition were truly a discarnate entity occupying an objective bit of time and space, then Mrs. Harbot should have said good-bye as the elderly woman she really was.

We must be careful not to become dogmatic in an area about which we know so little, however. Perhaps these images which come to say farewell to loved ones and to impart a bit of veridical information may be just what they seem to be—the truth-telling, leave-taking spirits of the beloved. Perhaps the mental machinery of Mr. Harbot, who suffered from hardening of the arteries, would have perceived his wife as a younger woman even if her discarnate soul had appeared to him in the form of the elderly woman she was at the moment of her death. How many of us have witnessed elderly grandparents addressing our parents as if they were still children, rather than the middle-aged men and women who stand there in the reality of the present moment?

The depths of the enigma of apparitions of loved ones

seen at their moment of death cannot be easily plumbed, and we may be plunging into an even deeper mystery as we next examine accounts of lovers who seem to have transcended the grave.

2. LOVERS WHO TRANSCENDED THE GRAVE

One of the great questions which men and women ask concerning survival after death is whether or not lovers are reunited in the spirit world. Then, almost in the same breath, they wonder if a lover who has passed over maintains his love for the surviving partner. And what if the survivor of the marriage or love affair finds another earthly lover? Does the deceased lover become jealous, or does he now exist beyond petty concerns of the flesh?

Alson J. Smith, author of *Immortality, the Scientific Evidence*, once spoke on the question of marriage in the spirit world and offered his opinion that he did not believe that two souls would be reunited as husband and wife. "I think they recognize and love each other," Smith said, "but marriage is an earthly institution with a physical basis; there is no need for such an institution or basis in the spirit world." It was Smith's personal belief that "husband" and "wife" were meaningless terms in the spirit world, for on such a plane of existence there would be only individuals who had achieved higher levels of understanding and deeper insights than they had known on earth. "The widow who remarries will be joined not only by her two earthly husbands, but by all who have achieved her level of understanding. It is only our physicalistic, limited thinking that makes this idea unattractive to us."

Although Chapter 3 will deal with accounts of jealous spirits which allegedly returned to torment their surviving love partners, it would seem, based upon the subjective as well as veridical proof offered by most of our haunted lovers, that the deceased mate maintains an affectionate interest in the one dearest to him who remains on the earthly plane. It may be that those reports which tell of discarnate personalities that remain jealous and possessive of their surviving partners deal with entities which are somehow held unnaturally to the earth plane by obsessive interests which have prevented their translation into higher spiritual strata.

The following account might serve as a typical example of a case wherein the spirit of a deceased lover continued to have a serious, although dispassionate, concern for the well-being of the surviving lover partner.

William Mandel and Eve Shields had known each other for several years and had become good friends long before they had begun to think of each other as potential sweethearts and mates. Their sudden awareness of each other as lovers had one day seemed a most natural thing, and they could not help chiding themselves for the three years of high school, four years of college, and two years working together in the same insurance company that they had wasted by not discovering particular facets of one another sooner. William would pronounce solemnly around the stem of his pipe that a Force-Greater-Than-They had seen fit to keep them apart, yet together, for nine years. Eve would sometimes blush at the memories of the many past occasions when she had taken her love-life problems to trusty William, who, at that time, had seemed like an older brother in whom she could confide.

When William proposed marriage, Eve did not hesitate

to give a positive answer. They had not fallen in love; they had grown in love.

Two months before the wedding, William was killed in an automobile accident.

"I was left to try to assemble the scattered pieces of what seemed to be a shattered life," Eve wrote. "It was nearly a year before I began dating again, but three months after I had begun to go somewhat steadily with Owen Laverty, he asked me to marry him. I was unable to give him an answer at the time, and I asked for a few days to consider his proposal. I felt that I could love Owen, but I also felt that I did not wish to marry him just then."

Eve explained her feelings to Laverty, but the man continued to court her for nearly two years. Finally Eve agreed to marry her persistent suitor.

Then, less than a week before the wedding, Eve recalled, "I lay tossing and turning in bed, unable to sleep. My mind was full of thoughts of William Mandel, my dead fiancé, rather than Owen Laverty, my living husband-to-be. My entire being seemed to be suffused with a strange uneasiness. How I wished that William might be there to discuss the matter with me, to give me sage counsel as he had so often in the past. In spite of myself, I began to weep.

"In between my sobbings, I was certain that I could hear William's voice calling my name. I sat bolt upright in bed, struck with the sudden realization that I was not imagining the sound of his voice; I was actually hearing William calling to me!

"I looked in the direction from which the voice seemed to be coming, and I was startled to see William standing solid as life next to my dresser. So many images began to flood my brain that I fear I nearly succumbed to the shock of seeing William standing there. Then I became strangely pacified at the sound of William's voice. 'Your marriage to Owen is a serious mistake,' he told me. 'You must not marry Owen Laverty. He is not the man for you. He is not what he appears to be.' "

Eve was so moved by the apparition of her dead fiancé that she feigned illness and told Laverty that they must postpone their marriage to give her time to recuperate. Two weeks later Owen Laverty was arrested on a charge of illegally possessing marihuana and such hard drugs as heroin and cocaine. During his hearing, evidence was produced which convicted Laverty of being a drug "pusher," a dealer in the illegal narcotics traffic. It was also revealed that Laverty was already married and had a wife in an asylum. The poor woman, whose existence had been previously unknown to Eve, had become a drug addict under the ministrations of Owen Laverty.

"Two years later," Eve wrote, "when Tom Shields asked me to marry him, I felt almost certain that an apparition of William Mandel, my dear friend and lover, would once again appear to let me know if my choice was a wise one.

"Three nights before our August wedding, William appeared in my room. He looked just as solid as he had when he materialized two years before. I was not shocked this time, and I waited eagerly for some sign of communication from him. This time William only smiled, waved a hand, and disappeared. I knew that dear William had given our marriage his blessing."

We should not leave this account before we make a brief note of the ability of one's unconscious to perceive matters which a neglectful and less aware conscious may not properly assess. In addition to feeling somewhat guilty for breaking her troth to the dead William, Eve may have heard bits and snatches of conversations and rumors which linked Owen Laverty to the illicit drug trade. Her conscious mind may have chosen to ignore these suspicions for a number of reasons, *i.e.,* a desire to be married and not remain single; an inner conviction that her love might reform Laverty; a secret sense of excitement regarding her suitor's criminal actions. On the other hand, Eve's unconscious mind may have remained incapable of being swayed by emotional arguments and may have assembled a portrait of Owen Laverty as he really was. In order to prevent an unsatisfactory marital union, Eve's unconscious may have externalized the apparition of her trusted friend and fiancé to outline the course of action which her own sense of morality had already convinced her inner self that she must take. Whether Eve accepted advice from beyond the grave or from her own unconscious mind, the phenomenon of seeing an apparition of her dead fiancé permitted her to make the proper decision which would ensure her future happiness.

Our next account in this chapter seems to offer a bit more veridical proof of a concerned lover who transcended the grave, but the desperate wife's recovery of lost money may have been the result of clairvoyance on her part. As the reader is learning, the more we discover about the limitless powers of mind, the more difficult it becomes to establish truly evidential proof of the intervention of a discarnate personality in the mundane affairs of our corporeal world.

In the March 1957 issue of *Fate* magazine Mrs. Minnie Harris told how her dead husband returned to pay the mortgage.

It was during the hard Depression year of 1932 that John Harris had his skull crushed by the wildly kicking hooves of their mule. John had just returned from town with ten crisp new one-hundred-dollar bills which he had withdrawn from the bank in order to pay off their loan to a money-lender they had nicknamed "Old Skinflint."

Mrs. Harris had forgotten all about the money until the undertaker had come to remove John's body. When she searched his clothing, she was shocked to discover that the envelope containing the ten bills was missing.

Her mother arrived, and the two women went over John's clothing inch by inch and searched the house, the closets, the cupboards, even the feed bins in the barn. Mrs. Harris trusted the neighbor who had helped her with John's body. She knew that Bill would not have stolen the money. Only one explanation remained: John had hidden the money just before he had been killed by the terrible hooves of the mule. "Old Skinflint's" note would be due in a couple of weeks, and he would foreclose and take the Harris home without the slightest hesitation unless the money was forthcoming.

A week before the note was due, Mrs. Harris received a curt, unsympathetic reminder from "Old Skinflint" that he expected the money on the appointed date. In continued desperation she searched under sacks of mash, beneath the straw in the hens' nests, in tool chests, but she could not find the one thousand dollars that would keep the moneylender from foreclosing on the farm.

Three days before the note was due, Mrs. Harris had a dream in which John came to her and tried to tell her where he had hidden the money. "But he couldn't speak because of his broken jaw," Mrs. Harris said. "As he turned sadly to leave the room, I screamed, 'John! John! Come back. Tell me where you put the money.' But he melted into mist, and I came awake in a cold perspiration to find Mother trying to shake me awake."

Mrs. Harris was half-resentful that her mother had awakened her. She was convinced that the spirit of her dead husband would have given her some clue if only she had been allowed to continue her dream.

The next night she sat up in bed late, reading her Bible, searching out all the verses which dealt with dreams and visions. When at last she fell into a fitful sleep, she saw John appear in the doorway and motion to her to follow him. Mrs. Harris screamed at him to wait for her; then she was abruptly awakened once again by her mother, who was standing over her.

On the third night Mrs. Harris went to bed with the conviction that John would once again return and attempt to communicate with her. She begged her mother not to awaken her no matter how loudly she might scream.

It was nearly dawn when the image of John appeared at her bedside, took her hand, and led her to the kitchen door.

"It had snowed in the night," Mrs. Harris remembered. "The rising sun was painting a rosy glow over the barnyard and fields. John pointed to his footprints leading from the door to the big haystack at the corner of the barn. Then he turned into a fleecy cloud and melted away like vapor before the sun."

Mrs. Harris found herself back in bed, the rising sun shining across her face. She threw on a robe, ran to the kitchen door. The newly fallen snow was smooth and unmarked, but in her memory of the vision, she could still see her husband's footprints zigzagging through the snow.

She paused only to slip on a coat and a pair of overshoes. Mrs. Harris found the money in a long tobacco tin which had been hidden deep under the hay.

The famous British novelist Charles Dickens, who brought the world his famous ghosts of Christmases Past, Present, and Future, as well as old Marley with his clanking chains, testified in his own words that he had experienced some personal encounters with the etheric realms. Dickens wrote how he awakened one morning to see the apparition of his father sitting by his bed. "As he did not move, I became alarmed and laid my hand upon his shoulder, as I thought; and there was—no such thing."

Dickens' most remarkable paranormal experience, and one more in keeping with the theme of this book, came to him after the death of his young, beloved sister-in-law Mary Hogarth in 1837. Dickens was terribly bereaved over Mary's sudden, tragic passing, and some of the novelist's biographers have suggested that Dickens had taken more than a brotherly interest in his wife's sister. Shortly after the girl's death, Dickens began experiencing nocturnal visitations from Mary's spirit, as the attractive apparition regularly invaded his dreams. The lovely spirit became, in

Dickens' own words, ". . . as inseparable from my existence as the beating of my heart is."

The entity stepped out of Dickens' dreams on at least one occasion. The novelist testified that he could not clearly see the face of the phantom that appeared before him, but he was convinced that it was his Mary. "I was not at all afraid," he wrote, "but in a great delight, so that I wept very much, and stretching out my arm to it, called it 'Dear.' I entreated it, as it rose above my bed and soared up to the vaulted roof . . . to answer me a question . . . touching the future life. My hands were still outstretched towards it as it vanished."

John Frederick Oberlin, the famous pastor, educator, and philanthropist, literally transformed the whole life of the Ban-de-la-Roche valley in the Vosges Mountains of Alsace. Shortly after the clergyman's arrival in the district, he expressed his immediate and earnest displeasure regarding the superstitions of the natives. Pastor Oberlin became especially agitated over the villagers' reports concerning the apparitions of dying loved ones. The new pastor resolved to educate the simple folk, and he launched a vociferous pulpit campaign against such superstitious tales.

In spite of his orthodox denial of apparitions, the reports of such phenomena continued unabated, and Pastor Oberlin was honest enough to admit that he was beginning to feel his dogma crumbling around him. In 1806 a dreadful avalanche at Rossberg buried several villages, and the reports of visions of the dying appearing to loved ones became so numerous that Pastor Oberlin at last came to believe that the villagers were indeed perceiving spirits of the departed.

In *Footfalls on the Boundary of Another World*, Robert Dale Owen tells us that Oberlin came to believe that his own wife appeared to him after her death. The clergyman maintained that his wife's spirit watched over him as though she were a guardian angel. Furthermore, Pastor Oberlin claimed that he could see his wife's spirit, talk with her, and make use of her counsel regarding future events. When a skeptic asked the cleric how he was certain that he could distinguish his wife's spirit communications from the fantasy of dreams, Oberlin replied: "How do you distinguish one color from another?"

Oberlin compiled extensive manuscripts which described in detail a series of manifestations in which his wife appeared to him and dictated information regarding life after death. Owen quotes a Frenchman named Matter who visited Pastor Oberlin to discuss his beliefs with him: "Oberlin was convinced that the inhabitants of the invisible world can appear to us, and we to them, when God wills; and that we are apparitions to them, as they to us."

A young woman who visited some friends in Milwaukee, Wisconsin, found out just how real those inhabitants of the invisible world can seem.

"Marilyn Erickson and I had roomed together for two semesters," writes Kathy Mueller. "When she invited me to her home to spend the weekend, I was looking forward to a fun time in Beer City. As it turned out, the Ericksons were teetotalers and were not interested in the brews that had made Milwaukee famous. I knew that Marilyn drank on campus, but obviously she observed her parents' prejudices when she was at home.

"Marilyn and I went to a movie, then came home and watched a late show on television before we went to bed. Maybe I wasn't going to live it up the way I had hoped, but at least I was going to get my rest. I had a nice big bed in an attractive guest room, so, I asked myself, who was to complain?

"Sometime during the night, I was awakened by voices coming from downstairs. They were strange voices, like people having a heated discussion, yet trying to hold their voices down. I have never been able to be as cool and aloof as the modern chick is supposed to be. I am, admittedly, a curious person. I got out of bed, walked partway down the stairs, and leaned over the banister so that I might see who was going at it in the living room.

"The house was dark, illumined only by a night light in the upstairs bathroom, yet I could clearly see the figures of a young man and a young woman seated on the large, flowered couch. At first I thought that the young woman was Marilyn, but on second look, I could see that the two women only resembled one another, like sisters. Even though the two figures were clearly discernible, there seemed to be a weird kind of fog surrounding them, a billowing mist.

"I heard things like, 'But you know we mustn't' and 'Dad would kill me if he found out' and 'You know we must wait.' It seemed to me that the age-old argument of the sexes was going on in the living room between Marilyn's older sister, who for some reason neither she nor her parents had ever mentioned, and an eager boyfriend. I am curious, but I am no voyeur. I decided to return to my bed.

"The next morning I asked Marilyn why she had never told me that she had a sister. Marilyn paled and asked me what I meant. 'Oh, come on,' I teased. 'She can't be that much of a black sheep. Where is she now? Is she still sleeping in her room? I'd like to meet her.'

"We were on our way down the stairs to breakfast, but Marilyn caught me by the arm and led me back upstairs to the guest room. 'We mustn't let Dad hear this,' she whispered.

"I could not comprehend why there was such mystery about the errant sister, until we were alone in the guest room. Marilyn told me that her older sister, Rachael, had eloped with a young man late one night more than seven years before. The two young lovers had been killed in a head-on automobile crash as they drove to Minnesota to be married. Marilyn had been only twelve years old at the time, but she could remember the terrible months of self-recrimination which her parents had rent upon themselves.

They had been so strict with Rachael and so disapproving of her boyfriend that they held themselves responsible for the young couple's decision to run away to get married. Since that terrible night, the voices of the two lovers had often been heard in the downstairs living room, where they had so often, during their troubled courtship, discussed their present problems and their hopes for the future.

"At first I could not believe what Marilyn was telling me," Miss Mueller concludes, "but I searched all the rooms and could find no evidence that Rachael or any young woman other than Marilyn lived in the Erickson home. When I persisted in accusing my friend of putting me on, she got out an old scrapbook and showed me pictures of the two girls when they were younger. A photograph of Rachael in a formal, smiling and ready for a prom, really grabbed me. I was certain that she was the girl I had seen in the parlor the night before.

"I guess Marilyn must have told her parents that I had seen the ghosts, or maybe they had lived with the troubled voices long enough, for I learned later that the Ericksons left their home in Milwaukee and moved to another city."

This author has seen a number of photographs on which the ghostly features of loved ones known to the photographer, or to his subject, have appeared. I am not referring to so-termed "psychic photography," some specimens of which are extremely convincing, but to spontaneous and informal snapshots on which spirit images have appeared.

A Mrs. M. O. from Chicago, Illinois, claims a veritable sheaf of such photographs. According to her testimony, her father's first cousin fell in love with him and died of a broken heart a few months after he married another woman. Before she passed on, the rejected lover promised that she would always be with him and that he would be made aware of her presence.

"It was not long after her death," writes Mrs. M. O.,"

that Father had some pictures taken of himself, and the image of his dead cousin showed up on all of them. On each picture, she was seen to be standing behind him with her hand on his shoulder.

"As long as my father lived, she showed up on every picture of him ever taken, and he had photos snapped everywhere from Chicago and Detroit to Jacksonville and Tampa."

May we conclude that these photographs constitute tangible proof of the spirit's survival after the death experience, or had the dying cousin's suggestion acted as the mental catalyst that activated the man's paranormal ability to psychically impress an image of his cousin on the negatives? Perhaps the occultist's admonition that "thoughts are things" may be true if the thought energy exerted is powerful enough and positive enough.

In a recent account brought to my attention, a woman, whom we shall call Mrs. Sinclair, suffered the loss of her husband shortly before their silver wedding anniversary. Mr. Sinclair had promised his wife that she would receive, first of all, a very special kiss for putting up with him for twenty-five years. Once he had declared his intention of delivering that magnificent kiss, he would run down a list of extravagant gifts which he would add to her anniversary booty. He varied the list of presents so often that all Mrs. Sinclair was certain of receiving from her husband was a truly remarkable anniversary kiss.

Just a month before their anniversary, Mrs. Sinclair received a call from a furniture store which presented her with the shocking and sorrowful information that her husband had just dropped dead of a heart attack while purchasing some new furniture for her.

The anniversary celebration turned out to be a day of mourning. Mrs. Sinclair's married children and many friends came to visit her and to console her, but when they had all left that evening, she was alone with an empty house and the gift which she had purchased for her husband.

Slowly she prepared for bed, dawdling over her coldcream session. When she finally turned out her bed lamp, she was astonished to see what appeared to be a pinkish disk approaching her. It continued to grow as it neared her bedside, until she could see that the disk had been transformed into the head of her deceased husband.

"His features hovered about four inches away from my face," Mrs. Sinclair said. "His head kind of wavered, like it was trying to come into better focus; then it was very still. There was a kind of illumination coming from his face, and I could look deeply into his eyes. Then he kissed me, a lingering, special kiss. I began to cry, but he gave me a wink and that whimsical smile that I knew so well. Then, as suddenly as he had appeared, he began to fade from my sight. Smaller and smaller he became, until there was nothing but that pinkish disk . . . and then there was nothing.

"My husband had kept his promise. I had received my special anniversary kiss."

Although some researchers may explain away the phenomenon reported by Mrs. Sinclair as an externalization of her loneliness and sorrow, the widow will always cherish that phantom kiss as her personal proof of survival.

In the previous chapter we discussed the theory that telepathy from a dying loved one might in some way be responsible for the apparitions which men and women have reported seeing of their departing dear ones. It may also be that, rather than actually appearing as an objective, independent entity, the discarnate personality might be capable of transmitting telepathic impressions to his surviving partner from another plane of existence. Such a phenomenon might be illustrated in the two following cases.

Mrs. Lorne from Austin, Texas, recounted how, on her husband's last birthday before he passed away, he had received two elaborately decorated cakes, one from the family, the other from an organization in which the Lornes were active. Mr. Lorne had retained a childlike enthusiasm for birthdays and holidays, and he had been enormously pleased by the special attention which he had received.

Mrs. Lorne's birthday fell soon after Christmas, and because she had come from a large family who had subsisted on a meager income, she had become accustomed to having her natal anniversary passed over without special notice. The situation had been remedied after her marriage, of course, but she teased her husband about receiving two extravagantly large birthday cakes when she had gone so many years without having received any cakes at all.

"This year I'll see to it that you receive two big cakes on your birthday," Mr. Lorne laughed. "Then we'll be even, Mother."

Mr. Lorne died one week later from a sudden heart attack, and it would have appeared that he had been freed from all earthly promises and commitments. Such, according to Mrs. Lorne, was not the case.

On her birthday, Mrs. Lorne sat quite alone, feeling very sad and depressed. None of her family lived near, and none of her friends knew the date of her birthday. Her husband had been several weeks in his grave, and there seemed nothing for her to do but to spend a night in solitude and misery.

But on that cold and icy night, a friend traveled across the city by bus to deliver a cake and a carton of ice cream to Mrs. Lorne so that they might celebrate her birthday. Mrs. Lorne's friend told her that she had just returned home from work when she had heard Mr. Lorne speaking to her as if he were in the room. He had told her that it was Mrs. Lorne's birthday and that she should hurry out and buy her a cake.

The two friends had no sooner finished the cake and ice cream when the young girl who had been boarding with

Mrs. Lorne since Mr. Lorne's death entered the front door carrying a box which contained a beautifully decorated birthday cake. Mrs. Lorne had not mentioned to the girl that it was her birthday, and the young boarder had never known Mr. Lorne.

"My husband had kept his promise," Mrs. Lorne said. "He saw to it that I received two special cakes for my birthday."

Whether the telepathic impulse was generated from beyond the grave by Mr. Lorne or whether the lonely widow herself somehow managed to broadcast an impression of her late husband's promise, two living agents were dramatically commissioned to fulfill the oath of a dead man.

Mrs. Lois Barker writes that she attended Communion the day after her husband had been laid to rest. "I had attended the early service that Sunday, and my thoughts were filled with anguish as I contemplated the long years ahead without my husband."

Mrs. Barker said that she then sensed a presence next to her in the pew, kneeling beside her. "I knew that it was my husband, but I did not turn to look. I did not want to do anything to destroy the impression I had of his presence. I wanted to hold on to the feeling that John had actually returned to take Communion with me."

When Mrs. Barker went forward to receive the sacraments at the altar rail, she felt that the presence of her husband walked with her. But after she had knelt to receive the wafer and the wine, she sensed that John had once again left her.

A few days later, when she was visiting with her priest, the clergyman told her that he had had a most unusual experience at the early Communion service that Sunday. "As I was turning to face the altar," he said, "I had the most peculiar feeling that your husband had come in and had knelt down beside you. When you walked to the altar to receive the sacraments, I had to blink my eyes. It almost seemed as though I could perceive a dim outline of John standing just behind you."

Again it must remain a moot point whether or not the spirit of a dead husband or the manifestation of a telepathic impulse caused both the widow and her priest to "sense" the presence of the deceased. Whatever the explanation, Mrs. Barker received spiritual comfort from the belief that her husband's spirit had joined her in church that Sunday morning to partake of a farewell Communion service with her.

Frank Overland returned from the Korean conflict an emotionally scarred and embittered man.

While he had been overseas, his wife had entered the hospital to have a lung removed because of a malignant tumor. Frank's kid sister, Ellie, had been minding his daughter, Jo Ann, and the two of them had been killed in an automobile accident as Ellie was driving to the hospital so that the child might visit her mother. When Joan, Frank's wife, learned of the deaths of Jo Ann and Ellie through an indiscreet nurse, the shock proved to be too much for her, and she seemed to lose the will to live. Since Frank's parents had died when he and Ellie were very young, the soldier had lost his entire family while he was in combat. Frank Overland had weathered some of the bloodiest campaigns of the Korean war, and his body had returned to the States without a scratch. It was his mind that had been mangled and bruised.

Overland received his discharge papers, toyed with the idea of reenlisting, then considered answering the call of an African nation advertising heavily in the European newspapers for mercenaries. A couple of men he had known in the Army approached him with the idea and tried hard to sell him on their plan of joining the highly paid professionals who fought for hire. The men were rough, violent men who loved war and killing. They were men with whom he had never associated while they served together, but now that he was all alone, Frank reasoned, why not grab the money and run. His rifle would kill as well as the next man's.

Only one factor caused Overland to hesitate to give his decision to the men. Before he had been shipped to Korea, he and Mel Witmer, Ellie's fiancé, had talked about opening a custom garage together. Overland found out that Witmer had been drafted shortly after he himself had been sent to Korea, but he had had no news from him since Ellie's death. Although he and Mel would one day have been brothers-in-law and they had liked each other from their first meeting, Frank did not know Mel's parents' name and address. Maybe if he could contact Mel and learn when he would be getting out of the service, he would get a temporary job in the hometown until Mel was discharged. On the other hand, shooting a rifle in Africa for a few months could bring a lot of money fast, enough money to put a down payment on a garage.

One Sunday morning Frank was sleeping late. He rolled over to see what time it was, then opened his eyes wide when he saw the solid image of Joan, his wife, standing at his bedside.

"She gave me her brightest smile," Frank wrote. "She was just as pretty as I would always remember her. 'Try to have courage to get through these bad days,' Joan told me. 'I am happy here. So are Jo Ann and Ellie. Oh, and Mel is here with us, too. He and Ellie came over together. We are concerned about your companions. We don't want you to go to Africa. We don't want you to kill anymore. We love you and we will always be with you. You are not really alone.' "

Before Frank Overland could speak, the vision of his wife had disappeared from his sight. "I wanted to hold her, to touch her, to talk to her, but it was like she just evaporated," Frank said.

Overland grew skeptical about the apparition as the day wore on. He had always been a hard-nosed pragmatist who had never believed in anything he could not hold in his hands and see with his own eyes. Perhaps, he reasoned, he had been too preoccupied with thoughts of his family's death and the question of whether or not he should join the men in their mercenary trek to Africa. The apparition of his wife had given him one bit of information which would prove to be disheartening if true, but which could be checked out if he could contact Mel Witmer's parents. According to the apparition, Mel was also dead and had died on the same day that Ellie had been killed.

At last Frank thought of a girl friend of Ellie's who worked in a neighborhood bank. Perhaps she could tell him more about Witmer. She and Ellie had been very close.

The young woman did know the names of Mel's parents and the suburb in which they lived. Frank called them that night and learned that Mel Witmer had been killed in action in Korea on the very day that Ellie and Jo Ann had been killed in the automobile accident.

Joan's apparition had told him the truth, and even though Frank Overland should have felt more alone than ever after learning of the death of Mel Witmer, he turned down the proposition of the mercenaries and decided to get a job and set about rebuilding his life.

"I'll always remember the words that Joan spoke to me from that vision," he said. " 'We love you and we will always be with you. You aren't really alone.' "

A medium recently told me of a woman who was in great distress and in need of money who had come to her for psychic counsel. The woman's husband had passed on suddenly, and since he had no insurance policies, he had left his wife and four children virtually penniless. It was a cold fall, and the winter would be even colder. The children needed new heavy clothing, and she needed money until she could find suitable employment.

"I had met this woman for lunch," the medium said. "Although I was not in trance and we were in a crowded restaurant, I could see distinctly an image of the woman's husband building up behind her. I described the man, and the woman verified that I must be seeing her husband. She began to weep, but I paid little attention to her. The man who was in spirit was telling me something very important.

"The man told his wife that he loved her and would cherish the memory of her and the children forever. He also said that he had not left her destitute. If she would go down into their basement and look behind the cabinet of old fruit jars there, she would find several loose bricks. If she were to pry them out, she would find three paid-up insurance policies in a tin box. There would be more than enough money there to provide for the children's education and to keep the family functioning comfortably until she was able to find a decent job.

"The woman was shocked. She knew of no such hiding place, and she knew of no insurance policies. 'I've never gone to a medium before,' she said, then hesitated. I could see that she was wondering if I was some kook just making up a story to tell her. Then the man in spirit spoke to me again.

"Your husband said that he was wrong to have kept the papers a secret, but he had been paying the premiums on them for several years and he regarded them as a nest egg for your old age or as a comfortable sum for you and the children if he should die. He knows now that he was wrong not to have told you about the insurance policies, but he died so suddenly that he had no time to give you this information.

"The woman left me shaken, pale, not entirely convinced. That night I received a telephone call from her informing me that I truly must have made contact with the spirit of her husband. She had looked behind the cabinet of old fruit jars, found the loose bricks, and discovered the insurance policies in a tin box. True to her husband's promise, she and the children would be comfortably situated."

Had the spirit of the woman's husband actually spoken

through my mediumistic friend, or had the medium exercised a psychic capacity of clairvoyance to discover the secret of the hidden insurance policies? Telepathy, unless the impulses were transmitted by a discarnate entity, must be ruled out in this case, because no living person knew of the location of the documents. When I suggested the possible utilization of clairvoyance in the discovery of the policies, the medium became quite exasperated with me.

"Look," she began, "first of all I had never met this woman before in my life, and I knew nothing about her except that a mutual friend had asked me to talk to her. Second, I had never known her husband or had any idea what he looked like on the earth plane. Third, I provided the woman with information which no living person knew —information which only the dead man could have provided. Good lord, man, what proof of survival will you accept?"

I can understand the medium's impatience and exasperation. As I have already pointed out, it has become a great paradox of psychical research that our ever-increasing knowledge of the limitless reach of mind has made conclusive proof of survival all the more difficult to obtain. In a day when man's inquiring mind was less sophisticated, less demanding, such a mediumistic coup as the production of "spirit-gained" information which led to the discovery of hidden documents would surely have been widely and unanimously hailed by all investigators as absolute proof of survival. Today, however, we feel compelled to ask whether or not some transcendent level of the medium's subconscious might not have penetrated a certain level of the subject's mind to gain past information (*e.g.*, physical description) about the woman's husband, and if the medium's clairvoyant powers might not have given the woman the information about the hidden insurance policies.

But, surely, reason does have its limits, and the medium

may have been quite justified in demanding of me, "What proof of survival will you accept?"

Dr. O. A. Ostby recorded a number of séances which took place over a seven-year period that not only provided a great deal of evidential material concerning a deceased young woman who purported to communicate through the various mediums, but also managed to reunite two haunted lovers.

According to Dr. Ostby, who wrote the account for the December, 1954, issue of *Fate* magazine, the image of a young girl who was in spirit appeared beside his chair sobbing hysterically during a séance in the fall of 1921. When he inquired as to the nature of her sorrow, the spirit asked him to write to the chief of police in St. Louis, Missouri, and ask for verification that a girl named Edna Ellis had been murdered there in the latter part of 1920.

A lady sitting in the circle promised "Edna" that she would write the letter, but the volunteer became busy with moving chores and forgot her promise. At the next meeting of the circle, the spirit of the young girl once again appeared and repeated her request.

Dr. Ostby wanted to know why the spirit desired that such a letter be written, and "Edna" replied: "Because that would help my people to think right about me. They think I was murdered because I was a bad girl, and that is not true!"

The spirit girl told the circle that she had had her throat cut from ear to ear by her sweetheart, George Ellis. "We had the same last name," she explained, "but we were not related."

The next morning Dr. Ostby wrote to the chief of police in St. Louis. It took several weeks before he received a terse reply that such a girl named Edna Ellis had been murdered in November of 1920 by her sweetheart, who was now serving a life sentence for the crime in the Missouri-state penitentiary.

Dr. Ostby attended a meeting of the spiritistic circle with the letter in his pocket, but he had been careful not to tell any other member of the séance group that he had received any reply from the St. Louis authorities. There were no secrets from "Edna," however.

"I see you got a letter from the chief at St. Louis," the spirit told Dr. Ostby. "I would like to make a correction, though. He uses the name Albert Ellis, while I gave you the name George Ellis. The truth is that his name is George Albert Ellis. I always called him George, but he was convicted under the name of Albert Ellis."

"Edna" told the group that she had now been able to appear to George in his prison cell and that he had asked her forgiveness for murdering her. "I have forgiven him, and all is well," the spirit said before fading back into the ether.

Dr. Ostby wrote comforting letters to George Ellis at the penitentiary and considered the matter closed. Then in the fall of 1922 he learned that Ellis' case had been reviewed by the Supreme Court of Missouri. George Albert Ellis was released because the police had used unlawful means to obtain his confession.

"In a meeting on July 16, 1928 . . . Edna Ellis again came to stand by my chair," Dr. Ostby writes. "When she spoke this time, her voice vibrated with joy and happiness. 'Doctor,' she said, 'I had to come once more to thank you for what you did for George and me. You were the means of leading us to the light.' "

A masculine voice came through the medium, identified itself as George, and thanked Dr. Ostby for writing to him while he was in the penitentiary.

Dr. Ostby concludes his article by stating his conviction that the spirits of the two young people had found everlasting happiness on a higher plane of existence.

We have already conjectured briefly about the likelihood of lovers retaining an interest in one another beyond the grave, and it should not surprise the reader that this question, like so many queries that touch upon intensely subjective and personal opinions, has a great deal of extremely dramatic documentation to prove either side of the argument. We shall be examining a rather substantial amount of such documentation throughout the course of this book.

According to the Spiritualist publication *Psychic News* (December 28, 1968), Sir Henry Segrave became curious about messages from séance rooms when he received a spirit warning which prevented a serious motoring accident shortly before he broke the world's speed record on land at Daytona Beach, Florida. Upon his return to Britain, Segrave attended a séance with a Spiritualist friend and saw such phenomena as a piano being raised from the floor with no one touching it. Such bizarre and unexplainable phenomena intrigued Segrave's engineering mind.

Not long after Sir Henry had had his interest in the paranormal considerably piqued, he was killed during another speed-record attempt. On the Sunday after Segrave's passing, his Spiritualist friend noted several spontaneous phenomena occurring in his apartment, and he became convinced that Sir Henry was attempting communication. The friend wrote to Lady Segrave with this information, but it was more than a year later before the widow attended a séance held under the mediumship of Estelle Roberts.

According to *Psychic News*, whose editor had been in attendance that night, the spirit trumpet moved to Lady Segrave and a voice issued forth which called her by a pet nickname which only Sir Henry had ever used. "Sir Henry made a valiant effort to communicate," the account states, "but obviously he had not learned the technique."

Lady Segrave became a regular attendant at the Estelle Roberts séances, and the spirit of Sir Henry became more adept at the mechanics of communication. Lady Segrave testified that the conversations which she held with her deceased husband were "as natural as if he was still on earth." She described the spirit messages as "very characteristic, full of intimate details, so that I knew beyond doubt it was my husband.".

Lady Segrave asked Red Cloud, Estelle Roberts' spirit guide, for permission to bring a stranger to the circle. Permission was granted, and the lady brought a close friend of Sir Henry, whose presence was acknowledged by the spirit's divulging of a number of personal details which only the two men had shared. Later Lady Segrave brought Sir Henry's brother and sister-in-law, and, according to Lady Segrave, "always the evidence stood every test."

At last Lady Segrave made public the story of her personal communication with her deceased husband. "I was a brokenhearted woman," she said. "Then I got proof of my husband's survival. Spiritualism removed all fear of death. It brought me peace and comfort in my hour of trial."

Peace and comfort may truly have been brought to Lady Segrave as a result of her attendance at Estelle Roberts' séances, but the question of whether or not the séances actually brought her the spirit of her husband will remain unresolved in the minds of many.

The problem of "proving" survival has many prickly thorns. As I wrote in *ESP: Your Sixth Sense:* "If an honest medium were to tell us that he has contacted the spirit of a close friend or relative who has passed away, what evidence would satisfy us that the 'spirit' was indeed who he claimed to be? If a discarnate voice reaches us via a long-distance telephone line, we accept the information that it is our friend calling from Alaska, because we know that he is alive and well. If, however, the same voice were to issue from the mouth of an entranced medium three years after our Alaskan friend had died, how would we determine whether or not the voice was truly that of the departed personality?

"I think that we should decide to be quite cunning and ask the spirit voice questions to which only our friend would know the answers. Intimate, highly personal questions, which would require a memory shared to be properly answered. Perhaps we would deliberately give an incorrect date or name to see if our spirit would notice the error and correct us. We should certainly be on the guard for peculiar mannerisms and idiosyncrasies of thought and speech which were representative of our friend's personality. We should also test the spirit's reactions to ideas and issues about which we knew our friend had strong opinions."

But the great paradox again looms before us. If the alleged spirit should pass all of our subtly devised tests with a perfect score, do we then accept this astonishing demonstration as proof of our friend's survival after death? Or do we again debate whether or not the entire astonishing performance might have been the result of the medium's remarkable control of such "extrasensory" phenomena as telepathy and clairvoyance?

In the next chapter we shall meet haunted men and women who care not one whit about academic paradoxes or about resolving the enigma of ESP versus the survival of the human personality. The tormented lovers whose accounts we shall next examine claim to have been beset by the jealous spirits of those whom they once loved in life before they were physically parted by death.

3. JEALOUS SPIRITS THAT TORMENT FORMER LOVERS

Dr. Loriene Chase, a clinical psychologist who maintains a private practice in Beverly Hills, California, writes a newspaper column dealing with psychological problems. Recently her column dealt with a husband who complained that his wife was allowing her life to be controlled by the dictates of a Ouija board. To complicate matters, the wife insisted that her deceased former husband was the spirit who was communicating with her via the board.

According to the complainant, he had married the woman ten months after her first husband had died. His wife and her late husband had been happily married, and their union had produced three little girls.

One day the oldest girl came home with a Ouija board. When his wife tried her hand at the tripod, the message she spelled out claimed to come from her deceased husband. The alleged spirit entity vowed that he still loved her and that he missed her. Soon the woman was weeping and talking to the board as if it were an embodiment of her first husband.

The woman's reliance upon the Ouija board progressed to the point where she had informed her second husband that they must obtain a divorce. She told him that she had known from the beginning that it had been a mistake for them to be married, for he was not at all like her first husband. According to the woman, her first husband catered to her whims and allowed her to run things the way she wished.

"It's possible that your wife feels a degree of guilt over marrying so soon after the death of her first husband or regrets the decision in some way," Dr. Chase said in answer to the man's query. "Add this to the fact you are 'different' and therefore unsatisfactory in your behavior toward her.

"If one or more of these factors are operative, it could be she has allowed these feelings to pyramid to the point where they have created the bizarre behavior you are now witnessing. The Ouija board would be her instrument as a way out of what she feels is a mistake."

From the viewpoint of a clinical psychologist, perhaps many of the reports which we shall examine in this chapter might be diagnosed as the manifestation of "a degree of guilt" which certain men and women have felt over marrying or courting others after the death of a mate or sweetheart. Indeed, unless one cynically wishes to conclude that all of the percipients of paranormal activity in this chapter are pathological liars, it seems that only two hypotheses can remain: (1) Conscious or unconscious feelings of guilt regarding infidelity toward a deceased mate or sweetheart have manifested themselves in bizarre and dramatic displays of psychic phenomena; or (2) the possessive, earthbound personalities of deceased men and women, confused by their sudden state of death, have remained to jealously guard their relationships with their surviving lovers.

In Kiel in northern Germany in the early 1920's a case of what appeared to be such a jealous ghost was well documented by the police, a number of university professors, and several psychic investigators.

Shortly after World War I a laundryman married a

woman who had had a child by a sailor who had gone down in the battle of Jutland. The first few months of their marriage were uneventful; then one morning when the husband sat down to his breakfast, a scalding cup of hot coffee leaped from the table and tossed its steaming contents into his face.

While the man reached in agony for a napkin with which to sop up the scalding liquid, assorted pieces of crockery and cutlery became animated and began to hop up and down on the table like popcorn on a griddle. As he shouted for his wife to come witness the phenomena, the lively saucers and knives and spoons began to launch themselves at his head. Unfortunately, he was unable to duck all of the suddenly hostile missiles from his breakfast table.

The laundryman staggered off his chair, bruised by a blow to his temple, and his chair shot to the ceiling and smashed itself to kindling. The abortive attempt of the chair to rocket into orbit above the city of Kiel rang down the curtain on the bizarre phenomena for a few days.

Act Two of the eerie drama took place one night when the man attempted the natural act of getting into bed with his wife. He threw back the bedclothes, reached out his arms to embrace his wife, and the bedstead split with a startlingly loud crack just inches from his ear. Before the astonished man could swing his legs out of bed, the mattress suddenly decided to emulate a magic carpet. The mattress elevated both itself and the wide-eyed couple for several inches, then dumped them onto the floor.

The discarded husband and wife were given no time to sputter conjectures as to the nature of the unearthly disturbance that had beset them. A large clothing cabinet toppled forward onto them, and the husband was barely able to get an arm up in time to prevent the heavy piece of furniture from crashing painfully against their skulls. He maneuvered to his knees, began to push the cabinet back to its original standing position. He nearly lost control of the piece when he heard his wife screaming. Turning his head to see what invisible monster had attacked from the rear, he was terrified to discover that the blankets on their bed were being consumed by crackling flames.

The couple decided that they had moved into a haunted house, but it soon became apparent that the increasingly vicious rampages were directed only against the husband. Whenever he entered a room, whatever object was closest to him would launch a direct frontal attack against his head. If he managed to sneak into a room seemingly undetected, the chair on which he would endeavor to sit would be jerked out from under him, and if he did not move fast enough, would be cracked against his poor skull. On several occasions, drawers which the man opened flamed up in spontaneous combustion.

The man and wife moved to a hotel, only to have their room become almost immediately transformed into an aggressively animated nightmare of wildly dancing furniture. They were forced to move from one hotel to another, then to a succession of rooming houses, as the phenomena and angered room managers evicted them from room after room.

Anyone who tried to investigate the mysterious plague found himself beset with similar woes. Policemen, professors, and psychical researchers had their clothes burst into flame or torn from their bodies. More than one officer was struck by some unseen aggressor. In one instance, a police car on the way to investigate the reported disturbances suffered three flat tires and two collisions within a mile.

At last one psychic investigator brought with him a medium of high repute. The medium in her entranced state told the couple and the assembled witnesses that the jealous spirit of the sailor who had been killed in action was responsible for the violent maelstrom of psychic activity. Since the medium had in some way received the impressions of the deceased sailor and the fact that the sailor, rather than the laundryman, was the father of the couple's child, it seemed to follow that her conclusion that the sailor's spirit was the couple's unseen tormenter was also correct.

The denouement of the case came when the laundry-man and his bride of a few months agreed to separate in order to save his life. Whether by an actual statement from the medium or by their own assessment of her entranced relay of information, the newlyweds had inferred that the sailor's jealous spirit would not rest until it had killed the usurper of his woman's affections.

Not long ago one of my correspondents sent me a report containing the reminiscences of a friend's grandfather who had suffered an attack from a possessive spirit. In this instance, the man's wife had died when very young, leaving the Kentucky farmer with a number of young motherless children. Before her death, however, the wife had warned her husband that she would not rest peacefully if he took another woman to his bed. The husband had promised his dying wife that this would not be so, but after a year of attempting to be both father and mother to his children, as well as trying to scratch a living out of the soil, the farmer decided that he must take another wife.

There was neither time nor money for the traditional honeymoon when he took his new bride, so the newlyweds simply drove from the church to the man's farm. As she prepared the bed that night, the bride took a lovely quilt from a cabinet and smoothed it across the rather worn bedspread.

"You gonna use that quilt on the bed?" the farmer asked, trying to mask his discomfort.

"Why, yes," his bride replied. "It is so beautiful. What intricate work. Who made it?"

"It . . . it's been in the family," the man mumbled. He wondered if she would read his thoughts, if she could fathom that the quilt had been made by his first wife? It had been a piece of needlework of which she had been exceedingly proud. Justifiably so, it seemed, when it had taken first prize at the county fair.

The farmer struggled w'th himself mentally. Should he tell his bride that his first wife had made the quilt and that it made him feel uneasy to see it lying there across the bed? Was it being disrespectful to use his dead wife's quilt to cover him and his new bride on their honeymoon night? Or should he heed his minister's advice and let the dead bury the dead?

His first wife *was* dead, he decided, crawling beneath the covers. He had made a promise to her that no fair-minded woman would expect him to keep. But still he felt uneasy, and he could not turn off the part of his brain that kept showing the pictures of his first wife as she lay dying and making him promise never to take another woman to his bed. Even as he reached for his new bride in order to consummate their marriage, the image of that dying woman seemed to lie there between them.

He was jolted back to the present by a woman's scream. He blinked his eyes, looked down in surprise at the woman who lay beneath him, screaming and pointing at something over his left shoulder. He turned his head, and his heart nearly stopped its beating. There, at the foot of the bed, was a shimmering image of a woman. It pointed an accusing finger at the couple in bed, then faded from sight.

As the frightened newlyweds lay in each other's arms, the only sensory impression that had managed to push itself through their fear was the fact that it was becoming inordinately hot beneath the covers. Their line of vision was finally distracted from the fading, ghostly figure by the thin tendrils of smoke that had begun to curl up from the quilt.

"The quilt is on fire!"

The farmer leaped out of bed, snatched the smoldering quilt from their bed. The moment it touched the plank flooring of their bedroom, the quilt burst into a brilliant ball of flame. Within seconds, nothing remained of his first wife's prize quilt but a few specks of soot and ashes. The jealous spirit of the farmer's first wife had apparently made certain that her quilt would cover no other occupant of her husband's bed.

Psychical researchers have long noted that the sexual adjustments of the marital state can trigger such phenomena as uncontrolled manifestations of psychokinesis, the direct action of mind on matter. Combine sexual adjustment with conscious or unconscious feelings of guilt, and one may find the impetus for a psyche's bursting free of the body's inhibiting three-dimensional bonds and utilizing virtually limitless mental talents, which may materialize other voices, other personalities, ghostly images, and the awesome power to, prismlike, focus enough energy to ignite fires.

G. T. B. from Cleveland, Ohio, had been married to Mr. P. for only a few days when objects began to disappear and to reappear mysteriously. Mr. P. was several years older than his young wife, who was not yet out of her teens, and he admitted that he had been married once before. According to Mr. P., his wife had died from blood poisoning after an operation. He had been a private kind of person who valued his solitude; yet he had soon become lonely and had been eager to remarry.

One night his wife awakened to find herself gasping for breath, an icy hand clutching at her throat. She grabbed the hand in desperation and tore it away.

"Are . . . you . . . try . . . trying to . . . strangle me?" she panted, shaking her husband awake.

It was apparent that the man was in a state of deep sleep. His eyes flickered open momentarily, and he mumbled, "It's in the black box," before he resumed his snoring.

"What's in the black box?" his wife demanded, shaking him angrily. But he was oblivious both to her demands and her tiny hands thudding against his thick body.

Mr. P., who had gained some reputation and considerable income as a brilliant, but eccentric, inventor, now set out to build his bride a new home. She, in turn, was eager to move, because she had concluded that the house must be haunted by some malignant entity intent upon strangling her. On a number of other occasions, she had awakened at night, gasping for breath, wrenching a cold, clutching hand away from her throat. After each attack, the only response that she could ever elicit from her soundly sleeping husband was, "It's in the black box."

"When we moved into our new home," G. T. B. recalled, "my husband had the movers place an old trunk up in the attic. He said it had belonged to his former wife. I was busy and paid little attention to it. I was never a very curious woman. The trunk remained unopened for several years, and our new home was also blighted with horrible manifestations."

One night as they sat reading in the living room, the couple was startled to hear a series of pitiful groans issuing from upstairs. Mr. P. grew suddenly pale, as if an invisible vampiristic phantom had instantly sucked out his blood.

"What on earth, or who on earth, is making such a dreadful noise?" the woman asked her cowering husband. She begged him to go upstairs and investigate, but Mr. P. sat dead still, firmly a part of his easy chair. He gave no indication that he had heard his wife. He sat repeating over and over again: "It's in the black box! It's in the black box!"

G. T. B. decided that she had lived long enough with midnight stranglings, awful groans, and an eccentric husband. Her mother came to stay with her for a few days, and G. T. B. discussed her husband's bizarre behvior, the eerie manifestations which followed them from home to home, and her decision to obtain a divoce. "I simply feel that I have lived with this situation long enough," she explained to her mother.

Her mother surprised her when she suggested that they

go up to the attic and open the trunk which Mr. P. had identified as having once belonged to his former wife.

G. T. B. was reluctant to pry into another woman's trunk, even if that other woman were dead, but her mother was determined that they might obtain some clue to the mystery among the belongings of Mr. P.'s former wife.

G. T. B. wrote: "We found that the trunk was not locked, and I opened the lid. We were greeted by the smell of musty clothes. Under the clothing I found a black lacquered box. 'Could this be that black box that your husband is always talking about in his sleep?' Mother asked.

"I opened the box and found a small urn filled with ashes. 'Her ashes!' Mother and I shouted at the same instant."

G. T. B. left her husband and later divorced him. She was convinced that the ashes in the crematory urn accounted for the thumps and moans which she had heard and for the cold hand that had tried to strangle her so many times in the night.

"Mr. P. had never buried his first wife," she remarked. "It was her anger at him and her jealousy of me that made her want to kill me or drive me out of the house. Hers was a most angry, restless spirit. I never found out whether he ever buried her ashes, for I left him soon after my mother's visit."

Anthropologist Walter Cannon spent several years collecting examples of "voodoo death," instances in which men and women died as a result of being the recipient of a curse, an alleged supernatural visitation, or the breaking of some tribal or cultural taboo. The question which Cannon sought to answer was, "How can an ominous and persistent state of fear end the life of a man?"

Fear, one of the most powerful and deep-rooted of the emotions, has its effects mediated through the nervous system and the endocrine apparatus, the "sympathetic-adrenal system." Cannon has hypothesized that, "if these powerful emotions prevail and the bodily forces are fully mobilized for action, and if this state of extreme perturbation continues for an uncontrolled possession of the organism for a considerable period . . . dire results may ensue." Cannon has suggested, then, that "voodoo death" may result from a state of shock due to a persistent and continuous outpouring of adrenalin and a depletion of the adrenal corticosteroid hormones. Such a constant agitation caused by an abiding sense of fear could consequently induce a fatal reduction in blood pressure. Cannon assessed "voodoo death" as a real phenomenon set in motion by "shocking emotional stress—to obvious or repressed terror."

Dr. J. C. Barker, in his collection of case histories of individuals who had willed others, or themselves, to death [*Scared to Death,* Dell Books, 1969], saw voodoolike death as "resulting purely from extreme fear and exhaustion . . . essentially a psychosomatic phenomenon."

In the next three cases which we shall examine, the jealous spirits undoubtedly killed by the voodoolike phenomenon of producing a state of shock within the percipients —but kill the apparitions did, either directly or indirectly.

In the October, 1963, issue of *Fate* magazine, Audrey M. Antkiewicz reported a story of a haunted lover who had been scared to death, the particulars of which had been witnessed by her husband when he was fifteen years old. The incident occurred in the tiny village of Ostrowice, Poland, in July, 1938.

Conrad Gizinsky was to marry Andzia Zalewsky on a bright Saturday morning. The young man had been engaged to marry Andzia's sister, Anna, just twelve months before, but the bride-to-be had died of appendicitis a few weeks before the wedding. The tragedy had touched the entire village, and everyone grieved along with the sorrowing Conrad. Now, all the villagers agreed, the young man could forget the tragedy. Andzia would make him a fine wife, and it seemed good that Conrad should marry the pretty sister of his deceased fiancée.

It was not unusual to have Polish wedding parties last for two or three days, and the bride's parents, Joseph and Marysia Zalewsky, did not intend their daughter's wedding to be an exception. After the ceremony, the festivities continued at their home, and everyone in the village had been invited to participate in the dancing, as well as partake of the food and the drink.

The nuptial celebration was at its peak at ten o'clock that night, and the lively strains of a happy Polish polka reverberated throughout the village streets. Everyone was in good spirits and vicariously savoring the joy felt by the newlyweds. The mother of the bride was sitting in a corner, chatting with a lifelong friend, Mrs. Zofia Szynkowsky, the aunt of Mr. Antkiewicz, husband of the contributor of this account. Mrs. Zalewsky glanced up to smile at the young people enjoying the polka, then felt her arm being clenched violently by her friend.

"My God!" Zofia Szynkowsky gasped. "My God in heaven! Marysia, see who is looking at the party through the window!"

The mother of the bride turned to look, and emitted a long, piercing wail. "There in the open window, clothed in a shroud and watching the proceedings with a sad expression on her white face, was her daughter Anna, Conrad's dead fiancée," Mrs. Antkiewicz writes.

It was as if some powerful hand had suddenly shut off the mortal switches of every villager in attendance. Everyone stood stock still, eyes widened, mouths opened in speechless shock and horror.

At last the bride's father shook himself free of the terrible spell and bellowed his rage at what he had assessed to be a cruel trick some thoughtless prankster sought to play on Andzia and Conrad. He snatched a powerful hunting rifle from a closet and ran outside. Several male guests followed the maddened father, some to restrain him and to prevent him from firing the rifle, others to shout their encouragement of his slamming some hot lead into so vicious a trickster.

"In the bright moonlight," Mrs. Antkiewicz writes, "they could see on the path about fifteen or twenty yards ahead of them the white-clad figure of a woman heading toward the nearby village cemetery.

"Mr. Zalewsky ordered her to stop, and when she did not, fired several shots. At that range he could not possibly have missed. The figure never faltered, but continued a few yards further, and then vanished. The men spread out and searched, but they failed to locate their quarry."

When the puzzled men returned to the Zalewsky home, they found the once gay party in a state of complete chaos. Andzia was in a state of shock, and a number of elderly ladies were hysterical. Andzia's and Conrad's wedding party did not last two or three days. It ended that night.

Andzia never fully recovered from seeing Anna's apparition at the window, and six months later she joined her sister in death. It seems that the ghostly image of her sorrowful sister had filled Andzia with guilt and an awful sense of betrayal. She lived in constant fear that the accusing specter of Anna would once again return and appear before her. Perhaps Andzia reasoned that the only way which she could rectify matters with her sister was to die, thereby removing herself from Conrad's arms in the same manner that Anna had been taken from his embrace. Once the suggestion had been implanted in Andzia's unconscious mind, she simply wasted until she died.

In 1715, Pedro Lemus, a prosperous merchant of Lima, Peru, hanged himself and left a most bizarre and sacrilegious will.

Just five years before, Sr. Lemus had emigrated from Spain with a young wife who quickly became famous in the new land for her exotic beauty and her exquisite features. Although he was envied by every man in Lima, no man could hate Lemus because of his reputation for fair business dealings and great personal piety. Señora Lemus, as well, was respected for her daily church attendance and her manner of carefully veiling her breathtaking beauty so that her presence would not prove to be too distracting to the devout males who knelt for Mass in her proximity.

Then, one morning in June, Pedro Lemus' chief accountant and a dozen employees found their master hanging from a beam in his study.

It seemed impossible to those who knew Sr. Lemus that the prosperous and pious merchant had committed the sacrilege of taking his own life. When the man's will was read, however, there could remain no doubt that Pedro Lemus had willingly performed that terrible insult against his Maker and that he had compounded the sin by adding most monstrous blasphemy. After Lemus' will had disposed of his great wealth by bequeathing sums of varying value to every employee and distant relative, the document emphasized the woeful fact that the beautiful Señora Lemus would not receive a single coin.

"I bequeath my soul to the devil," Pedro Lemus had scrawled in a bold hand, "provided that he shall destroy my wife and Don Gonzalo Ramírez y Ponce, who have become intimate lovers."

Beside his firmly underlined signature was a drawing of a Holy Cross with a dagger driven through it to the hilt. The tormented man had hereby proclaimed his emphatic renunciation of the Father in Heaven and of all His saints.

While the others present at the reading of the will stood about gasping at the shocking revelation that Pedro Lemus had delivered from beyond the grave, the wife of the mayor, who was a close friend of Señora Lemus, left the group and hurried to the nearby home of the widow. She demanded that she be allowed to see Señora Lemus at once, but the servants professed their ignorance as to her whereabouts. The mayor's wife stood fuming in the entryway, impatiently stamping her foot. She had wanted to break the news of Pedro's will to her friend before the executor and the various witnesses arrived; but now, as she gritted her teeth angrily, she could hear the accountants and the others at the door.

The entire assemblage was able to hear the terrible cry which arose from the Lemus' gardener. The frightened man had come upon the bodies of a naked woman and a partially clad man in his lady's small, vine-covered summer house in the garden.

Upon investigation, the servants and employees of the Lemus' household and business, together with the Lemus' friends and city dignitaries, found the woman to be Señora Lemus. The man, whose cold arm stretched across Señora Lemus' naked bosom, was Don Gonzalo Ramírez y Ponce. the captain of the viceroy's guard. The spark of life had been long extinguished in both the lady and her lover, and strangely enough, neither body bore the slightest mark upon it. A subsequent inquiry found no evidence of poison, and the official inquest concluded by offering Pedro Lemus' will as final proof that the two lovers had been killed by the devil in exchange for the soul of the cuckolded merchant.

It must be remembered that the zeitgeist of Lima, Peru, in 1715 was completely dominated by a fanatical kind of religiosity. All of art, business, architecture, even the exploitation of the native Indians was performed with one hand upon the cross. No one, cleric or cashier, virgin or demimondaine, missed daily Mass. Each cipher in the accountants' books, each social function, each public or private affair, awaited the edicts of Mother Church. Surely such an overabundance of religious fervor must bestow new and fiery life in the devil, he who tempts, as well as accomplishing an almost morbid fear of God, He who judges.

One might, depending upon his personal bias, conjecture that Don Pedro's deal with the devil set in motion a fearsome life-squelching curse, a bundle of negative thoughts and hatred that actually claimed the lives of his unfaithful wife and her lover. On the other hand, one might wonder if the betrayed husband might not have spewed out his terrible curse in a personal confrontation with the lovers, and that their own unconscious minds, convinced of the terrible power and validity of a pact with Satan, literally scared themselves to death. Perhaps the wrathful Don Pedro might even have declared a time limit, stating that upon his suicide that night, and the delivery of his soul into Satan's eager hands, all the fiends of hell would come for their deceitful bodies.

In his book *Scared to Death*, Dr. Barker lists a number of well-documented cases in which men and women died on the appointed due date of a hex or curse because of their conscious or unconscious fear that they *would* die on the predicted dates. Dr. Barker expresses his opinion that, in certain cases of deaths resulting from premonitions and predictions, the victims died from autosuggestion. "Initially the subject develops the notion that something is going to happen; then this idea operates through autosuggestion so as to bring about the very thing which was anticipated. We have already become familiar with the powerful consequences of suggestion, which can have particularly harmful effects upon the subject's state of health. It would be difficult to dismiss the death [in the case he cites] as being due to natural causes. If death was occasioned by other agencies, they were certainly not apparent."

A conviction of guilt and a sudden bone-chilling fear may also become the lethal ingredients which can frighten a person to death, and may, in some strange psychosomatic way, actually create bizarre physical evidence of ghostly murder.

Jim Daniel of Logan County, West Virginia, was among the first of the American troops to land in France in 1917. At first his letters came regularly to Darlene Mastin, his girl friend, but then all correspondence from Jim's end ceased. Darlene continued to write to him, however, for she reasoned that it had to be very difficult to write letters in the trenches. What Darlene did not know was that Will Daniel, Jim's older brother, had been intercepting all of Jim's letters to her and destroying them.

Will was also in love with Darlene, and his passion had led him to become so desperate that he had resorted to such low tactics as hiding all of Jim's letters in the hope that Darlene's ardor toward her absent suitor would cool. In addition, Will would stop by Darlene's home and talk at great length about how soldiers behaved away from home and how seductive the French "mademoiselles" would appear to a simple country boy. When Darlene ignored his suggestions and remained faithful to Jim, Will dipped into his bag of dirty tricks and came out with the foulest deception of all: he faked a telegram which stated that Jim had been killed in action.

It seemed touching, commendable, and quite natural that Jim's older brother should be at hand to console Darlene in her anguish, to pay her court, and, eventually, in October of 1917, to marry her. Although Darlene had never considered Will Daniel as a suitor and had been very much in love with Jim, it somehow made Jim's passing less difficult to accept, knowing that the man on earth closest to her dead sweetheart would make her his wife.

According to the documents which record the principal testimonies in the case, Darlene was in the kitchen preparing Christmas Eve supper when she heard the front door open and the unmistakable sound of Jim Daniel's voice.

"It's a dirty thing you done to Darlene and me," she heard Jim tell Will, her husband. "I know all about how you worked things so you could get her, and I'm going to kill you the way you deserve!"

The mountain people of Logan County do not make idle threats. The man she had loved and thought dead was in the front room, and he had just threatened to kill his brother, the man she had married. Darlene felt flushed and dizzy. It was painfully and immediately apparent that Will had either made a terrible mistake or had deliberately lied to her about Jim's death. She wiped nervous hands on her apron. Whether Will was innocent or guilty of an unforgivable deception would have to be judged later. Right now, she must go out to face Jim, because there was no denying that he was very much alive and had come home from the war.

Before she could enter the front room, the blast of a gun thundered through their modest home. Darlene ran into the room just in time to see the back of a uniformed man go out the door. Will Daniel lay sprawled grotesquely on the living-room floor. There was an ugly, bleeding hole in his forehead, and a look of fear and disbelief in his staring eyes.

Darlene stood numb, immobile. There were so many horrible things churning around in her mind.

When a series of sharp knocks sounded at the door, she went to open it as if she were an automaton. A boy with a telegram stood there, leaning lazily against the doorjamb. Then he looked beyond Mrs. Daniel to see the grisly scene that lay behind her, and he ran off screaming for the sheriff without waiting for the woman's signature on his pad.

No one knows if Darlene Daniel, in her state of shock, was able to comprehend the contents of the telegram at that particular moment, but the evidence the telegram contained remained for all to examine and to ponder. The message had been sent from the War Department, and it was terse and direct: "To William Daniel. Regret to inform you that on December 21, 1917, your brother, James Daniel, was killed in action in Germany. . . ."

The authorities took an exceedingly dim view of Darlene Daniel's story that the spirit of the wronged brother had come back to Logan County after his death and had killed her husband for revenge, but the facts remain that investigating officers found no evidence that anyone other

than the Western Union boy had been to the Daniel residence that night. In addition, no murder weapon was ever
found, and it could be proven that William Daniel had
never owned any kind of firearm.

Sometimes, it appears, the possessive spirits of former
lovers only want to receive a last bit of recognition from
their living mates before they leave them in peace and
advance to higher planes of existence.

Shortly before her marriage to Brian O'Donnell, Ellen
Sterling was warned by some of her fiancé's friends that
Margaret, his deceased wife, had sworn that she would
haunt him if he should ever remarry. Ellen thought the
statement in excessively bad taste, but she simply smiled
and expressed her wish that Margaret would understand
and leave them in peace.

On their first night in Brian's home after their honeymoon, however, Ellen began to reconsider the women's
idle chatter from the standpoint of an ominous prediction
that had been realized.

They were just preparing for bed when they both heard
a violent thumping from the room that Margaret O'Donnell had occupied in the last months of her illness. The
woman had suffered a stroke and had been left unable to
speak. Whenever she wished something, she had been
forced to knock on the wall to call attention to her needs.
It now seemed to Ellen, as they stood there listening to the
loud, thudding sounds on the wall, that Margaret wanted
something: she wanted Brian O'Donnell's new wife out of
the house!

Brian mumbled something about a loose shutter, but
Ellen noticed that he was very pale and visibly shaken. At
last he breathed a deep sigh, as if he firmly regretted the
age-old tradition that made it incumbent upon the male of
the species to investigate all strange night noises. He fas-
tened the belt of his bathrobe securely about his waist,
then stepped out into the hall.

Ellen sat nervously on the edge of the bed. She had resolved to give up smoking, but Brian's pack of cigarettes on the nightstand was about to be looted. Then the noise, the terrible pounding, stopped.

She turned to glance at the door and was startled to see a colorless, bony hand reach around the doorjamb and shut out the lights. She sat on the edge of the bed screaming until Brian entered the room and snapped on the lights.

There were no further manifestations that night, but Ellen told her husband the next morning at breakfast that she did not want to sleep another night in that bedroom. Brian agreed and said that as soon as he returned from work that night he would help her move the furniture to a back bedroom.

Brian had not been out the door a minute when a flurry of knockings and thumpings sounded throughout the house. The venetian blinds shook as if they were caught in a heavy breeze. Ellen was certain that she could hear the sounds of things being moved about in the attic.

"At that time," Ellen wrote, "I did not think that I would be able to go on living in that house. There was something living in dark shadows that did not want me there. For several days the pattern never varied. There would be the thumpings at bedtime, the knockings and scrapings during the day. On a number of occasions, as I worked in the kitchen, I heard what sounded like a sick person dragging her feet up the stairs. Whenever I would push open the kitchen door and look up the stairs, however, there would never be anyone there."

Ellen had tolerated the eerie manifestations for over a week when, one day, she heard a loud pounding from Margaret's bedroom. She put down her sewing and glanced up the stairway. There had been a departure from what she had come to accept as part of the haunting's regular schedule. Up until that time, the pounding from the bedroom had sounded only at bedtime.

Ellen continued to watch the top of the stairs. If she had

not known that she was alone in the house, she would have sworn that there truly was an invalid in that bedroom who was trying desperately to signal her. The longer that Ellen concentrated upon the sounds, the more that she became convinced that the spirit of Margaret was actually attempting to communicate with her.

"I'll never know how I managed to summon the courage to do so," Ellen admitted, "but I walked up the stairs and entered the bedroom where Margaret had lived her last days. I don't know what I expected to see. I guess I thought that I might be confronted with the ghostly image of the poor sick woman whose place I had taken.

"The room still had an antiseptic smell to it, and it had received only a cursory cleaning after Margaret's death. I stood there in the middle of the room, not really having the faintest idea what my next move might be.

"A loud thud sounded next to the bed where the dying woman must have lain and rapped out her pitiful signals to the part-time maids that Brian had barely managed to afford. I turned quickly, nearly losing my balance. An envelope seemed to flutter down from somewhere like an autumn leaf dropping from a tree. I picked it up, saw that it was a letter which Margaret had written to Brian. It was sealed, and from all appearances had never been opened and had never been read by the man to whom it had been sent.

"That night I showed the letter to Brian, and hesitantly he took the envelope from my hands. Tears streamed unashamedly down his cheeks as he read the letter.

"When he had regained his composure, he told me that Margaret must have written the letter just hours before her death. In her own words she told him how much she loved him and that she prayed that he would forgive her for some of the selfish and thoughtless things which she had said in bitterness at the onset of her illness. When she had been deprived of her voice after the stroke, Margaret had written, she had been forced to do more listening and more thinking. She hoped that he would remarry if she should die, but she begged him to always remember her with kindness and to think only of the good days which they had shared."

According to Ellen O'Donnell, she and Brian still live in the same house, but she has never again heard the eerie knockings and the strange thumpings from Margaret's old room. "I don't really think the surviving personality of my husband's first wife was trying to drive me away," she wrote, "but I do think that she wanted to make her position clear to me and to Brian. It was as though she would not permit, or sanction, our marriage until Brian had read her last letter to him."

According to Mrs. B. H. of California, the spirit of a deceased lover appeared to her so that it might enjoy a last laugh at her expense.

W. J. had been much older than she when they married. In fact, W. J. was several years older than her father. "W. was a real jealous sort of man," Mrs. B. H. wrote, "and it wasn't very long before I charged mental cruelty and divorced him. I was probably too young and flighty for marriage, anyway, but I married again before I was out of my teens."

Mrs. B. H. had not heard any news of W. J. for over a year, when one night, as she and her second husband lay in their upstairs bedroom, the image of W. J. appeared at the foot of their bed.

"He just stood there looking down at us," Mrs. B. H. remembered. "I kept thinking of how jealous I had made him and how I had hurt him, and I was fearful at first that he had broken into our house to do us harm. But he just stood there looking at us, and then he started to laugh. He didn't say a single word, but he must have stood there laughing for nearly a minute. Then he turned and ran down the stairs."

Mrs. B. H. and her husband were completely stunned,

and several minutes passed before either of them could speak. "What in hell was that?" her husband demanded, more of his powers of reason than his equally startled wife.

"That . . . that was W. J., my first husband," she told him. "But how or why, I can't tell you."

Sleep was next to impossible for the remainder of the night, but that next morning at breakfast, Mrs. B. H. found at least a partial answer to the mystery of the apparition in the daily newspaper. "We read that W. J. had passed away just a few moments before his spirit had appeared in our bedroom."

Mrs. B. H. was still puzzled that the image of W. J. had been laughing. Such an apparition certainly did not fit into the stereotyped version of a mournful figure in a flowing white robe.

She did not have long to wait for an answer to her enigma, however. Her second husband confessed to her not long after the spirit of W. J. had appeared in their bedroom that he had been seeing another woman and that he had fallen in love with her. He asked to have his freedom.

"It was now apparent to me why W. J. had materialized in our bedroom and had stood laughing over us," Mrs. B. H. wrote. "He was getting a good last laugh at me. He had been terribly jealous of me, as jealous as I was toward my second husband, and I had left him, just as my second husband was about to leave me. There I was: married and divorced twice, and I was not yet twenty."

A few years later, Mrs. B. H. married again, this time successfully. "Maybe W. J. destroyed my second marriage," she conjectured. "Maybe he decided that I should not find happiness until I had suffered at least one terrible heartbreak."

There seems to be yet another category of spirits who return to haunt their former mates, but these entities, if such they be, are much more benign, and rather than being termed "jealous ghosts," should rather be referred to as spirits who have maintained a somewhat proprietary interest in their earth-plane love partners.

When her husband died in the fall of 1944, Dorothy Barnes of Vermont found herself beset with the many problems that a widow inherits upon the death of her mate. Since Dorothy had two children under four years of age, her most immediate problem had to do with finding enough money to keep them all eating. Her husband had left only a minuscule estate, as far as his insurance policies went, but he had bequeathed her a section of timberland.

"A certain gentleman from the community made an offer which seemed fair to me," Dorothy said. "I knew that he had a reputation for pulling some rather slick deals, but I didn't think that he would try to take advantage of a young widow."

In his last days, as he had lay dying of cancer of the stomach, her husband had been unable to sleep at night. In those restless and painful hours, he would lie at Dorothy's side and gently stroke her hair. The night before Dorothy was to close the deal on the timberland, she lay in a light sleep, mentally debating the wisdom of her actions.

"I had not been sleeping long," she recalled, "when I became conscious of a hand stroking my hair. I knew that my husband was still watching over me, and I felt prepared to handle any situation."

Dorothy awakened convinced that she should not sell the property. "I found out later that just the timber on the land was worth more than the price the man had offered me for the entire section of property."

The young widow struggled for over a year, trying to make ends meet; then she was forced to the painful decision that it might be better if she boarded her children and temporarily set out alone to get a good job and to save money so that they could all be reunited as soon as possible. She found a young couple in a nearby city who had six or seven children already boarding with them and who seemed to be the ideal kind of temporary foster parents for her two children. Dorothy had made all the necessary arrangements with the man and woman, and all that remained for her to do was to deliver her children early the next morning.

"That night, as before, when I had been undecided about the sale of the land, I felt my husband's steady hand caressing my hair," Dorothy said. "I awoke knowing with the utmost certainty that I must not leave my children with that young couple. I knew that I must not go ahead with my plans to board them. Only a few weeks later, I read in the newspaper that the couple had been arrested for ill-treating the children in their care and for feeding them spoiled food."

After four years had passed since her husband's death, Dorothy found herself in a position wherein she was seriously considering remarriage. "It was no secret to me that Bob indulged in more than a social nip, but he seemed quite able to handle his drink. Oh, I had seen him drunk on more than one occasion, but I rationalized this by saying that everyone got a little tipsy once in a while."

She had nearly made up her mind to answer "yes" to Bob's entreaties, when, one night, she again felt the caress of her dead husband's hand. Dorothy changed her plans, reluctantly at first; then she experienced the knee-weakening sensation of a narrow escape when Bob's father called her to confess that Bob was an alcoholic and had already spent one expensive session of several months' duration in a hospital.

"I later found out that the ever-vigilant spirit of my husband was not really jealous or possessive of me," Dorothy wrote. "For a time there, I thought that his presence would never allow me to marry, that his caressing hand would always come to find fault with any man who courted me, but such was not at all the case. I have now been happily married over twenty years. The beloved ghost of my first husband was only looking after me until he could safely leave me to fend for myself."

When Mrs. M. W.'s husband died, she left the Midwest and moved to California, selling nearly everything she owned in the process. For a little more than a year she was unable to obtain any kind of steady employment; then, finally, she decided to reactivate some old skills, and she found work as a laboratory technician in a small medical clinic. Four years later, one of the doctors, who had obtained a divorce from his second wife, asked Mrs. M. W. to marry him.

Mrs. M. W. considered the man to be charming, but she had never felt entirely at ease with him. The longer they dated, the more Mrs. M. W. doubted if she really loved him and if she should marry him. After a great deal of mental debate, Mrs. M. W. at last accepted the doctor's proposal of marriage.

One night, shortly before their wedding date, Mrs. M. W., unable to get to sleep, sat up in her bed reading. Then: "I noticed a strange radiation around the typewriter that I had left out on a desk across the room. I glanced about the room, trying to discover what could be casting such a peculiar glow on that particular spot. I tried to go back to my reading, but I found myself strangely attracted to that glowing glob of light. Then I heard the sound of typewriter keys being struck.

"I got out of bed and walked toward the desk. There, seated before the typewriter, his hands on the keys, was my late husband. I raised a hand as if to touch him; then both he and the strange illumination disappeared.

"I turned on the light, removed the sheet of paper from the typewriter. The spirit of my husband had typed these words: 'Don't marry the doctor . . . he will cause you heartbreak, sorrow. . . .' "

Confused, Mrs. M. W. told her fiancé that she needed more time to think, and she asked that their wedding date be postponed. The doctor reluctantly agreed to her terms, although their relationship became somewhat strained. Then, within a few months, the doctor killed himself in a fit of despondency over heavy gambling debts. Although he had somehow managed to keep it a secret from his colleagues in the clinic, the doctor had been a compulsive gambler.

The orthodox psychologist may assess Mrs. M. W.'s story as being the fantasy of a lonely woman who feared the re-establishment of an intimate relationship with a man; the psychic researcher may analyze the spirit writing of her husband as having been but Mrs. M. W.'s own automatic writing in which she unconsciously typed out her inner fears; but Mrs. M. W. herself will always believe that her husband's love had survived the grave and had enabled him to return to warn her of an inadvisable union with another man.

4. THE HAUNTED MARRIAGE BEDS
OF MEDIUMS AND PSYCHICS

"But, darling," the new bride protested, "I can't. I mean, I can't with . . . with *her* watching us!"

The impatient husband, whose ardor boiled briskly, mumbled that nothing must interfere with the consummation of their marriage.

The bride pushed her husband away and tried her best to clear his lust-clotted brain. "But *she* is watching us. How can we make love with an audience?"

The man sighed, rolled over on his back. "But I've told you, *she* is not in the body. She can't really care about concerns of the flesh."

"But then why does she scowl so whenever you reach for me?" the bride wanted to know. "And why does she look so pleased with herself now that I've put you off for the tenth time tonight?"

"Well, *I'm* not becoming very pleased with *you!*" the man growled loudly.

"Don't shout at me," the bride retorted. "She belongs to you, not to me!"

The man slid his legs from beneath the covers. His wife was right. Natasha was his spirit guide. She was his responsibility. And although he would never admit it to his wife, he knew that Natasha was jealous of his love for a woman of flesh and blood.

"Natasha," he began, getting to his feet and advancing toward the wispy, ethereal figure who stood at the foot of the nuptial couch. "Natasha, this *is* our wedding night. And, ah, we would like to have a little, ah, privacy. You know. You remember about such things, don't you? You see, when you just stand there and watch us like that, you upset Carol, my bride. So would you mind just, you know, disappearing?"

Slowly the spirit guide faded from sight, until only the wavering image of her petulant face remained; then that, too, disappeared.

"But she's still in the room!" Carol said. "I know that she's still here watching us."

"Sure," her husband agreed, "but at least you can't see her now."

This time when he reached out to take her in his arms, Carol acquiesced. After all, she decided with a deep sigh, which her husband mistook for passion, she would just have to get used to being married to a spirit medium.

The case histories recounted in this chapter will leave many a skeptic either sadly shaking his head at the state of delusion which some simpleminded souls accept as reality, or bent over double with laughter at the gullibility of this author in accepting as valid the experiences which have been reported to him by psychics, mediums, and their spouses. I shall avoid presenting a philosophical treatise on "What Is Truth," and I shall, at this time, sidestep the psychological geneses which may have prompted such phenomena as those which have been described to me by my paranormally gifted sources. According to their own testimonies and the supporting testimonies of a number of their friends who witnessed certain of the manifestations, these experiences actually occurred.

None of the sensitives I know on a close personal basis support the popular conception of the medium as a wild-eyed, bizarrely attired individual who has a great deal of difficulty establishing a successful presentation of normalcy. With the exception of a few male mediums with beards and a few female sensitives who favor large rings, anyone would pass these psychically talented men and women on the street and immediately evaluate them as solid members of the Silent Majority. And, indeed, a good many of the mediums whom I know personally are quite conservative politically and are genuinely disturbed and concerned that the social mores are in a period of flux and transition.

The first thing that any serious investigator of psychic phenomena learns is that mediums are people. They are nurses, accountants, journalists, real-estate agents, advertising executives, editors, housewives, ordained ministers, engineers, farmers—in short, one is likely to find as wide a range of occupations among mediums as he would find among people who are left-handed.

The case histories in this chapter shall be presented without a great deal of theorization on my part. The psychics who contributed to this chapter told their stories in a straightforward manner, and that is how I choose to present them. Because of the personal and intimate nature of the accounts, I shall, as I promised, change the names of those people who were actually involved in attempting a satisfactory adjustment to the haunted marriage beds of mediums and psychic sensitives.

The wedding-night scene with which we opened this chapter would seem humorous to all but the principals involved. The bride, whom we have called Carol, soon learned that her difficulties with Natasha, her husband's spirit guide, would not be confined to an occasional invasion of privacy of their conjugal relations. Natasha began to annoy Carol by tossing plates and cups about the kitchen. Once when Carol had finished a letter to her mother, the stamped and sealed envelope burst into flame.

Carol complained to her husband. "You've got to do something about Natasha. She's driving me mad!"

Although Carol had not been a spiritualist, she considered herself open-minded and understanding enough to be a suitable marriage partner for the handsome young medium. Before her marriage she had attended a few séances at which her husband had served as channel, and she had been favored by an apport of lovely roses. According to those in the circle, the flowers had been a gift from Natasha. Apparently, Carol now reflected, that had been before the spirit guide had realized that her channel was becoming serious about a woman of flesh and blood.

One night as the couple prepared to make love, the medium was ingloriously pushed out of bed by an invisible hand. On another occasion, Carol was slapped viciously across the face just as she was approaching sexual climax, and she was left feeling frustrated, unsatisfied, and seething with anger at her unseen rival. The spirit guide seldom materialized, but when she did, she appeared only as a scowling, petulant woman.

At last the distraught Carol sought the advice of another medium, a woman whom she admired for her practical wisdom, as well as her psychic talents.

"I'm afraid that your husband has not been completely honest with you," the medium told her. "Many brides have had difficulty adjusting to their husbands' spirit guides, but the bond between your husband and Natasha is a very strong one. You see, they have been together in many incarnations, sometimes as mother and child, sometimes as brother and sister, but most often as lovers. They are destined to be always together; only, it seems, Natasha was somehow omitted from the wheel of return for this incarnation. In this incarnation, she serves as his spirit guide, and she bitterly resents any woman who tries to usurp her physical position with him."

Carol had been reared in an orthodox religious background, and she was the graduate of a business college. She had always considered herself an extremely practical and down-to-earth young woman. Although she did not know if she could completely accept such talk of past incarnations and jealous spirits, she did know that the manifestations which occurred in their bedroom were a very real part of a situation which she had come to regard as intolerable.

Carol decided to bear the physical attacks of her unseen rival for only a short time longer. She made her decision to terminate the marriage one night when her husband was out of town and she awakened, gasping, wrenching a pair of partially materialized hands from her throat.

One of America's leading trance mediums told this author how her first marriage had ended in divorce because of her husband's inability to cope with the manifestations that haunted their marriage bed.

"My husband worked hard during the day and needed his rest at night," she recalled. "Those pesky spirits seemed to realize this, and they would visit us nearly every night at bedtime."

The manifestations would generally begin with a tugging at the bedclothes. "Damn it," the man would bellow. "Tell your devils to leave us alone."

As if they were mischievous children just waiting for such a reaction, they would seize the covers and tear them from the bed, leaving the couple bereft of their bedclothes. "On more than one occasion," the medium said, "my husband would get out of bed and grab his shotgun. There would actually be the sound of running footsteps, like they were afraid of him and were retreating from the room.

"With a war cry, he would chase them down the stairs and out the door. Then, just when he thought he had them chased away, he would hear them thumping around back upstairs. Some nights the poor man would run up and down those stairs until he would just collapse exhausted into bed.

"I used to live in mortal fear that one night one of the children would get up to get a drink of water and be shot down by accident by their father with his gun.

"The greatest blow to me came when I returned home from work one night and discovered that he had burned all of my books and my personal notes relating to spiritual work. He considered that such things were of the devil, and he hoped that he might rid the house of the 'demons' by burning all my materials related to psychic matters. I was afraid for a while that he would decide to add the 'witch' to the pyre as well.

"That night the spirits were at him so bad that I knew that we would have to separate in order to protect his life."

What is it like being married to a man who may be the outstanding medium in the world today, a man who can control psychokinesis [mind over matter] to such a degree that he is literally a modern Merlin? I brought such a question to his wife of little more than a year.

"To answer that question best," said the attractive brunette, "I'll have to start before our marriage, during our courtship.

"On the nights when we had a date, the furniture would start dancing about my room anywhere from several minutes to several hours before his arrival. Drawers would open, sometimes just as I was about to reach for them. Other times they would close after I had removed the item which I had wanted.

"I often thought that these manifestations must have occurred because he was visualizing me moving about in my apartment, getting ready for our date."

She told me that now, after marriage, the sensitive sometimes tunes in on her from his office. "It's like the apartment is psychically bugged." She laughed. "It is impossible to keep a secret from him.

"He has come home from the office and repeated, word for word, conversations which I have had with my girl friends.

"Once I wrote a letter whose contents I did not want my husband to know about. It was an angry letter to a man who had begun to take advantage of my husband's good nature. Then I thought better of the whole thing and ripped the letter to shreds. When he returned from work that night, he told me precisely what I had written and expressed his pleasure that I had decided not to send the letter."

To this woman, levitating furniture, animated catsup bottles, and tapping tables have become a way of life. To her great credit it must be said that she is among those relatively few long-suffering mates who have adjusted to living with a psychic spouse. Even as I write this, a letter from this couple has arrived, describing a series of strange materializations and dematerializations of household objects that even has the paranormally gifted husband baffled. It would appear that he is not responsible for these manifestations on either a conscious or unconscious level, but his devoted wife is confident that he will be able to determine their source through his remarkable psychic abilities.

Sarah Woodward married a rancher who lived in the Southwest. The rancher had been a widower for several years, much to the perturbation of his friends and their wives. He was a tall, ruggedly handsome man who owned a comfortable spread of grazing land. Matronly cupids in the area had been trying to play matchmaker for him for so long that they had almost given up on the eligible bachelor and stamped "not interested" across his forehead.

When he returned from a trip to St. Louis with his new bride, Sarah, the neighbors held a happy chivaree for them, and his friends' wives felt that once again all was right with the world. The women left the newlyweds alone, happily clucking about what a quiet, soft-spoken, and sensible woman Sarah appeared to be.

Sarah did, indeed, possess all of those wifely virtues, but in addition, she was the possessor of a secret which she had not told even her husband. For several years prior to her marriage, Sarah Woodward had been a spirit medium. Just a few months before she had met the tall, handsome rancher, Sarah had decided to disavow her mediumship. She had found the physical and mental drain of mediumship to be too great for her rather frail constitution, and she had grown weary of watching the eligible men pass her by in favor of more orthodox mates.

Now, more than ever, Sarah thought, as her husband took her in his arms, she was glad that she had decided to keep her mediumship a secret. She would not have wanted to scare this man away, even though his rugged features made him appear that he would not be frightened of anything.

But Sarah was soon to learn that her handsome rancher had also harbored a secret.

They were preparing to retire for the evening when Sarah was startled to see a woman walk unannounced into their bedroom. The woman stood motionless for a few moments, obviously seething with rage. Sarah looked at her husband, expecting him to speak to the woman, but he seemed to be unaware of her presence.

Sarah was admittedly unfamiliar with the local customs in the Southwest, but it seemed to her that invasion of privacy was rude no matter where one lived. This woman had no business storming into their bedroom, and Sarah decided to take it upon herself to tell her so.

"What do you want in this room?" Sarah demanded of the stranger. "All the guests have gone home!"

Her husband turned to her and laughed. "They sure have, and I guess you know what I want in this room. We're still kind of on our honeymoon, aren't we?"

Sarah blushed. "We're not alone," she told her husband, who still remained oblivious to the woman's presence. The woman had put her hands on her hips and had begun to tap an angry foot on the hardwood floors.

Her husband turned around in surprise. "I don't see anyone. What are you talking about, Sarah?"

It was true, Sarah realized at last. Her husband could

not see the woman, because she was in spirit. Sarah had only time to shout a warning before the angry, uninvited visitor from the spirit plane hurled a vase at her husband's head. He fielded the heavy glass vase on his shoulder, and it crashed to the floor.

"Watch those glass splinters with your bare feet," Sarah screamed above the din that had suddenly broken out in their bedroom. The spirit of the woman had gone berserk, and she had begun to fling and to topple anything movable.

"Louise! Louise!" her husband wept. "Please stop!"

At last the violent psychic storm had abated, and "Louise" left the bedroom. The rancher knelt on the floor weeping. He had taken blow after blow on the head and shoulders from bottles, brushes, and shoes. The bedroom furniture had been toppled, and some of it had been broken. The bedclothes were scattered about the room as if they had been caught up in a miniature tornado.

"She has a nasty temper, doesn't she?" Sarah said at last.

"She warned me that would happen if I ever remarried," the rancher said. "I've known she was in the house. I've felt her presence off and on for these seven years since she died."

Sarah nodded. He did not have to tell her these things, for she had already received strong psychic impressions that had told her everything, but it did him good to talk about it. "Well," she said, "she's one redhead who really lives up to their reputation for angry outbursts."

As soon as she had spoken the words, Sarah regretted having opened her mouth. Her husband looked at her quizzically. "How did you know she had red hair? None of the women tonight would have told you about her—or did they?"

"No," Sarah admitted. "I . . ."

Her answer was cut off by her husband. "You acted from the very first as if you could see her. You were talking to someone in the room before the disturbance began. Sarah," he demanded, "could you see her?"

"Yes," Sarah answered. "I could see her."

"But how? I've felt her sometimes. I heard her once or twice. But I've never seen her. How . . ." Her husband's hands made futile gestures in the air before him; then he fell silent. The night was quickly becoming more than his psyche was capable of digesting all at one time.

"Darling," Sarah began. "I've always been able to see men and women like Louise. Ever since I was a little girl."

"You can see ghosts?" her husband asked. His voice sounded as if it had come from within a deep cavern. He had righted a chair, and he now slumped weakly against its back.

"I can see men and women who are in spirit," Sarah replied. "A woman such as Louise has remained earthbound because of her possessive nature. She is strong and proud, and she was taken from you when she was young. What people call 'ghosts' are usually the restless spirits of those who died violent deaths and cannot adjust to their sudden change of condition; or, in some cases, they are men and women who are tied to the earth because of deeds left undone or because of earthly attractions that remain too strong."

Her husband leaned forward, cradled his head in trembling hands. She had not intended to say so much. She knelt and began to pick splinters of glass off the floor.

"Sarah," he spoke at last. "Can . . . can you *talk* to ghosts, too?"

She thought for several moments before she answered his question. "I am . . . I used to be what is called a spirit medium. I had given all that up before I married you."

"But you could see Louise?" he reminded her, bringing the full force of his red-rimmed eyes to bear on her.

Sarah had already considered this. Somehow she had known that the gift of mediumship could not be surrendered so easily. Somehow she had known that her renunciation of a talent nurtured within her psyche by forces outside of herself could not be accomplished in the same manner that one resigns from an employment situation with which he has grown weary and uncomfortable. She would be a medium until whoever had blessed, or blighted, her with such gifts decided to withdraw them.

Her husband took her hands within his own and clasped them with his strong fingers. She knew what he was going to ask before he had found the courage to voice the words. "Could you . . . talk to Louise and ask her to leave us alone? I once loved her, but . . ."

He could no longer speak, but Sarah understood. He was a lonely man of flesh and blood who sought to make a new life for himself with a new bride. The wispy, evasive companionship of an earthbound spirit could hardly suffice for such a man.

Sarah walked the hallways of the ranchhouse that night, but she could neither see nor sense any sign of Louise. She searched every room in the sprawling house, but it soon became obvious to her that the angry spirit of Louise had spent its wrath for that night. Whatever unknown forces had given her the strength to remain within the walls of the ranchhouse had been at least temporarily dissipated by the violent manifestation in the bedroom.

Sarah told her husband that she was quite certain Louise would return again the next night when they prepared to go to bed. As an earthbound spirit, Louise felt most jealous about the relationships with her husband which were the most intimate, the ones she would least wish to have him share with another woman. Certainly neither Sarah nor her husband felt like making love after such a vicious psychic attack. Louise had won the first round, and Sarah was convinced that the jealous spirit would return the following night to be certain that her husband would not enjoy conjugal privileges with a woman of material substance. Sarah's prediction proved to be correct. As she and her husband were undressing, Sarah caught sight of Louise striding angrily into the room. The spirit shook an angry

finger at the rancher. Sarah knew that the psychic fire-
works were about to begin again.

"Louise!" she shouted. "Listen to me!"

The spirit turned to her with a look of shocked surprise.
"You shameful hussy!" Louise snapped. "How dare you
speak to me? You come into my home like some common
slut and try to take away my husband."

"He's my husband now," Sarah replied softly. The spirit
had crossed the room and now stood eye-to-eye with her.
Sarah could see the terrible hurt and angry churning behind the spirit's eyes.

"What do you mean, *your* husband!" Louise shrieked.
"Just because that man, that no-good lug, had the audacity
to bring a whore home with him from St. Louis, he doesn't
need to think . . ."

"Louise," Sarah interrupted her, "you are in spirit! Stop,
think; you know that you are no longer of flesh. Remember
the day you died, the day they buried you?"

The spirit put its hands to its ears. "Stop it! Stop it! Or
I'll scratch your eyes out!"

"This is no longer your home," Sarah went on, speaking
in a soothing tone. "It is time for you to pass on. You
should have moved on seven years ago. You need not
worry about your husband. The concerns of the earth plane
now mean nothing to you. Remember your loved ones with
affection, but don't try to hang on to them. You must now
be concerned only with things of the spirit."

Sarah continued to speak in a soft voice of Louise's passing, of her necessity to accept the world of spirit, until, at
last, Louise dropped her hands from her ears. "That's why
he has not touched me for these seven long years. It was
so unlike him. He was always so affectionate. Then he just
stopped touching me. . . ."

The spirit turned to look sadly at the confused rancher,
who sat on the edge of the bed. He had been in the process
of pulling off a boot when Sarah had begun speaking. He
still sat with a hand on his boot heel, frozen, immobile,

fearful lest some movement, some small sound, might break the connection Sarah had established with the spirit world.

Louise began to weep. "I remember now," she said. "The minister standing over me. 'Ashes to ashes,' he said, and all my friends and relatives were standing there to agree. But I wouldn't believe it. I wasn't ready to leave. There was my husband, the ranch, the hard times I knew were coming. I had to stick by him and help him. These two old men came and said that they would guide me, but I told them to go to hell."

"Those men were your spirit helpers, your guardians," Sarah explained. "You should have gone with them. You should have realized that it was time for you to pass on."

"But I had to stay with my husband," Louise sobbed; then, the anger flaring again, "but he rewards me by bringing you home!"

Sarah put up a forefinger to hush Louise's outburst. "Remember, you have been in spirit for seven years. It is not good that man should live alone."

Louise scowled. "He had me, didn't he?" But this time her anger could not last. Her image was beginning to waver. Realization of her actual state of existence was beginning to pervade her being.

"He had you while you were in your material body," Sarah said, "but now you are in spirit."

"Now I am in spirit," Louise echoed.

A brilliant glowing orb formed behind them, and Sarah could make out the forms of two men standing within the golden light.

"They're here again," Louise said. "The two men are here again."

"Are you ready to go with them this time?" Sarah asked her.

Louise nodded. "Be a good wife for him," she said.

Before Sarah could reply, Louise had stepped into the orb of golden, glowing light. Sarah caught a glimpse of two men with white beards, of a landscape of rich green grasses and multicolored flowers, and then there was nothing before her but her husband on the edge of the bed, still holding on to his boot heel.

The medium whom I have called Sarah eventually re-entered the Spiritualist ministry with the blessing of her rancher husband. When she told me her story, she was in her late seventies and living in a nursing home in California, still alert, still studying, writing down experiences taken from a lifetime spent on the threshold between two worlds.

5. GHOST WIVES, PHANTOM SWEETHEARTS, AND SEX BEYOND THE GRAVE

Someone once said that all brides are beautiful, and Sarah Catherine Eaton certainly did her best to keep such a sentiment wholly intact. Sarah had remained a maid until the age of thirty-three, a state of affairs which had caused her friends no small concern; but now the lovely young woman stepped forward in an elegant satin dress with a veil and a bouquet of orange blossoms to meet her groom, Benjamin Pierce, son of the former President of the United States, Franklin Pierce.

The date for the nuptials was June 20, 1879; the place, the Leavenworth, Kansas, home of Sarah's parents, Colonel and Mrs. Isaac E. Eaton. After the ceremony, the newlyweds moved through the home, which was crowded with guests, to sit down among friends and relatives and partake of a wedding supper. The bride looked radiant, and the groom, attired in black broadcloth suit and white vest, retained a dignity befitting a son of a former President. In all ways but one, the Eaton-Pierce nuptials could stand as a typical Midwestern marriage celebration, *circa* 1879: Sarah had been dead since she was a three-week-old baby, and Benjamin had been killed in a railroad accident when he was twelve.

The Leavenworth, Kansas, *Times* for June 25, 1879, printed details of the slightly unorthodox wedding rites—Emanuel Swedenborg, Scandinavian clergyman who died in 1772, performed the ceremony—and the June 29 edition of *The New York Times* also carried a report of the spirit wedding. Colonel and Mrs. Eaton claimed that they had been in communication with their daughter since shortly after her death on November 20, 1845. Through various Spiritualist mediums, the Eatons had been able to keep in contact with Sarah during her childhood and adolescence, and they had been proud parents as she grew to maturity in the spirit world. Colonel Eaton and his wife reacted quite as normally as any pleased parents would when Sarah told them that she wished to be married to Benjamin Pierce.

The Leavenworth *Times* commented that Colonel Eaton had never made a secret of his Spiritualism, and such religious beliefs had not hampered him in becoming a long-time member of the National Democratic Committee. "It is well known to the public that Colonel Eaton, of this city, is a Spiritualist, and in this, as in everything else, he is thorough—he does no halfway business," the news report stated.

On the day of the wedding, two mediums entered a cabinet set up in the Eaton home, and combined their psychic energies to materialize the spirit forms of Sarah and Benjamin. According to the Leavenworth *Times:* "The announcement was soon made from the cabinet that the spirits were ready. The guests, one after the other, were invited up to the aperture [of the cabinet], where the lady and her husband were . . . receiving the guests very pleasantly."

After Pastor Swedenborg had blessed their marital union, the newlyweds left the spirit cabinet and took the places reserved for them at the wedding-supper table. The *Times* carried statements from those in attendance at the wedding who testified that Sarah and Benjamin took part in lengthy conversations with the assembled guests. The just-married couple spoke in great detail concerning their life in the spirit world before they took leave of the wedding celebration to return to the etheric realms for their honeymoon.

In fitting observance of the union of two politically prominent families, the social page of the Leavenworth *Times* published the guest list of those who had attended the wedding. Among those guests whose names were listed were several long-departed American statesmen and relatives of the ghostly couple.

On June 20, 1920, forty guests watched Pearl and Thomas S. Macquithey renew their marriage vows on the date of their twenty-second wedding anniversary. There was a special, solemn demeanor among the assembled friends of the couple on this anniversary observance, because Pearl Macquithey had been dead for two years.

Raymond Ross, writing in the March, 1956, issue of *Fate* magazine, reported that the ceremony took place in the home of Dr. H. Robert Moore of Dayton, Ohio. After the spirit of Mrs. Macquithey had materialized, Dr. Moore led the radiant woman to her waiting husband and daughter, who stood on the other side of the room. Mr. Macquithey embraced his wife, and Dr. Moore assisted them in the renewal of the sacred vow which they had made twenty-two years before on that date.

Ross quotes a statement signed before a notary public that reads: "We are able to affirm this, and that Pearl Macquithey was the same person who has appeared to us on each occasion. We have always been able to see her distinctly, and the room has had all the light possible to be had on such occasions. No person, at this or any other meeting, has been in the cabinet [the spirit cabinet from which the materialization issued], nor has any person at any time been in what is called a trance state. Mr. and Mrs. Macquithey and their daughter, Delphine, who acted as bridesmaid, stood before us during the ceremony, as stated in the foregoing, after which each of us was called in turn to extend our congratulations.

"We, the undersigned, were present at the twenty-second anniversary of the marriage of Pearl V. Graham with Thomas S. Macquithey, at the home of Dr. H. Robert Moore . . . Dayton, Ohio, First Speaker of the Psycho-Science Church. Mrs. Pearl V. Macquithey, who passed away October 10, 1918, has appeared to us (also to other friends) many times during the past year."

In his conclusion to the article, "Spirit Bride, Mortal Groom," Ross writes that he met Mr. Macquithey nearly thirty-five years after the man had renewed his marriage vows with a wife who was in spirit. According to the elderly man, he still received regular visits from the surviving personality of Pearl Macquithey, and he was looking forward to the day when he would walk with his bride on the "other side."

Although "spirit weddings" and "spirit renewal of vows" might be interpreted as the desperate manifestations of loneliness and rather esoteric religious practices, such ghostly ceremonies are not as uncommon as the reader might suppose. I have talked at length with individuals who not only claim to have maintained a physical relationship with departed spouses, but who insist that they have fathered or mothered "spirit children."

"My husband was taken from me shortly after we were married," one woman told me. "Our greatest desire had been to have children, and now that desire would be denied us. I knew that I might remarry, but I sincerely did not want to. I had loved John with all my heart, and I had wanted only to bear his children and be a good wife to him."

Then, one night as she was retiring: "I felt his arms around me and I knew that those were his lips at my neck.

I turned and beheld a very dim, wispy outline of my husband. His eyes were very easy to distinguish, and I identified him by those sparkling, lively green eyes. Later, when we lay down together, I knew without a doubt that it was John who was making love to me in his spirit body."

A short time thereafter, the woman noticed with joy that her womb was beginning to swell. Her menstrual periods had ceased, and she had begun to suffer from morning sickness. She quit her job, fearful lest the other secretaries would gossip. Who would understand how she had come by her condition? She went to live with some friends who were Spiritualists, and she contributed to her support by doling out sums from John's insurance money.

At last the nine-month gestation period had been terminated, and her friends prayed that a spirit doctor might come to accomplish the delivery of the child. In all that time, the expectant mother had not visited an orthodox gynecologist or general practitioner. The town was small, and she would not tolerate slanderous statements being made about her condition. She had literally become a recluse and had not ventured out of her friends' home since she had entered it.

She was told by her friends that their spirit guides were bringing a doctor with them and that her time was very near. The woman went to boil some water and tear some rags so that she might assist in the delivery as midwife. The birth pangs began, and the mother-to-be began to whimper in pain.

"When the baby was delivered," she said, "I could only see a tiny, smoky-looking glob, but I could see the image of John standing there, all smiles. My friends' guides told me that my baby would be taken to the spirit world where he would receive the best of care. Since that time, I have spoken to both my husband and my son on several different occasions when I have attended séances. It is so comforting to me to know that someday I will be able to join my family in the beyond."

The phenomenon of pseudo-pregnancy, which distends the womb and inflicts the woman with all the myriad discomforts of a normal period of gestation, is not unknown to the medical world. The will to believe can exercise a far greater control over one's body than the average man or woman might suppose.

Another woman told me of having borne a son who was composed of flesh and blood, rather than soul and ectoplasm, after sexual union with her deceased husband.

"Bill came to me in the night no more than four days after we had laid him in the ground," she told me. "He was rough in his lovemaking, brutal, like an animal. It was Bill, all right. I was so scared. He was at me all the time when he was alive. I figured he wouldn't ever leave me alone now that he was a ghost and would never have to rest."

The lusty spirit of her dead husband appeared just twice more, then disappeared forever, she recalled. But Bill's wild seed had found fertile ground, and she became pregnant.

"I didn't know how such things could be, but there was no arguing with my condition. When the boy was born, I named him after his father, because I figured that was the way Bill would have wanted it," she said.

To her dismay, Bill, Jr., grew to be the image of his coarse father. "I have always believed that his father's spirit came to possess that boy," the woman remarked with conviction. "He wasn't more than twelve years old when mothers started complaining to me about how he was pestering their daughters. When he was fifteen, he got arrested for stealing cars. They sent him to reform school, and when he got out he tried to kill me with a hammer. They got him locked up again now, but I figure when he gets out, his daddy's spirit is going to keep that boy after me until I'm in my grave."

As I talked with the woman, it occurred to me that her unconscious mind might have been aware that she was pregnant before her husband had passed away. Such unconscious knowledge may have become externalized in a vision of her husband's ghost making love to her, or she may have experienced a particularly vivid dream, which had accomplished the purpose of making her aware of her pregnancy. It struck me that this woman had been afraid of her husband, and she had not been the epitome of the grieving widow when he died. She may have had feelings of guilt, because, secretly, she may have been relieved that her husband had been killed in the accident in the train yards. The element of guilt may have intensified the image of the apparition, and its brutal treatment of her body may have been unconsciously designed to serve as a kind of penance for her failure to grieve.

The sensitive sponge of her son's psyche may have been aware of her unconscious hostility toward him from the moment of his birth. The mental chaos that such impressions would foster within a growing boy were probably responsible for his antisocial behavior and his hatred of his mother. For the woman herself, however, no explanation other than her Bill's return to father a devilish son will account for the fact that her boy is in an institution for the criminally insane.

Although it may seem unlikely that nonphysical spirits might be interested in performing acts of physical lovemaking, this author has encountered numerous men and women who testify to having had sexual encounters with lovers whose corporeal bodies lie in their graves.

"One woman told me that she felt her husband was a better lover after he had passed into spirit," a medium related not long ago. "In life, he had been cursed with premature ejaculation, but now, according to his widow, he can last and last."

"Charlie died when we were just kids in junior high," a young woman told another medium, "but I started seeing him standing beside my bed a couple of years later. Finally,

I let him come under the covers with me, and pretty soon we were making it. I wish I never would have let him, though. He was a lot better than the man I later married. Sometimes when my husband is gone, I feel like trying to see if I can bring Charlie back to me. I figure it's better that I don't, though. I don't suppose it would be like being unfaithful, having sexual intercourse with a ghost, but I never really did feel right about it."

Are the above statements, regardless of how sincerely they may have been expressed, really examples of sexual psychopathology? Sexual repression, frustration, loneliness, and confusion may breed a whole stable of psychological demons to delude men and women who may have become mentally disoriented due to shock, sorrow, or sexual deprivation.

But then there are the cases wherein evidential material was gained and the manifestations were witnessed by second and third parties, and one's whole cabinet of pet theories comes crashing down about his ears.

When Mrs. Helen Murad was a teen-ager, she moved out into the country and left her friends back in the city. In those days, school buses did not travel far beyond the city limits, and Helen found herself attending a country school. Every couple of weeks, Helen's mother would take the children back to their hometown to obtain books at the library. Helen was completely removed from her old school friends, except for an occasional chance meeting among the quiet stacks of the library.

About a year after her family had moved to the country, Helen quickly selected the books she wished to check out, then sat on the library steps to await her mother's return.

"I had not sat there long," she recalled not long ago, "when I saw a familiar figure approaching me. It was Peter, a boy with whom I had gone to school a year before we moved. He was a handsome boy, and all of the girls always made such a fuss over him. He was a good athlete, and he stood square with the guys, too.

" 'Hey,' he said when he spotted me on the steps, 'it's Helen. Hey, boy, have you gotten prettier since you moved. Must be that country living!'

"I blushed and was putty in Peter's hands. I offered little resistance when he asked me to walk across the street to the park and sit on a bench with him. He put his arm around me, and even though my heart started thudding so hard it hurt, I could take it. But I thought I would faint when he bent down and kissed me on the cheek!

" 'I always liked you, Helen,' Peter said. 'I was sure sorry when you moved out to the country.'

"I told him that I had missed all the kids at first, but my new friends in the country school were nice, too.

" 'Yeah, well, that's good,' Peter said, suddenly becoming rather glum. 'I'm going to go away, too.'

"My heart sank. I had just been creating the most beautiful mental pictures of Peter and me writing love letters back and forth and meeting when I came into town, and I even had a perfectly gorgeous image of seeing Peter drive down our lane in his old car. 'Where,' I asked reluctantly, 'are you moving?'

" 'Far away, kid.' He sighed. 'Far, far away. You ain't never gonna see this old boy again!'

"I felt terribly depressed, and I thought for certain that I was going to cry.

" 'How about another kiss?' Peter asked gently. 'A good-bye kiss.'

"This time Peter kissed me on the lips, and he held the kiss so long that I thought I surely would faint this time. When he finally let me go, I looked up into Mama's scowling face. She grabbed me by the hand, and I just barely had time to wave good-bye to Peter over my shoulder before Mama dragged me off to the car. I talked to Mama all the way home, trying to make her not be angry with me. When I explained that Peter was going to be moving away, she became somewhat more understanding and sympathetic, although she let me understand that she did not approve of any daughter of hers smooching on a bench in a public park."

It was nearly a month before Helen got back to the library. Illness and farmwork had prevented her mother from taking the children into town any sooner, and they knew that the books would have overdue fines on them. One of Helen's former classmates was working at the library desk, and as Helen doled out the fines, she could not resist telling the girl how she and Peter had necked in the park a few weeks previously.

"That's bad taste, kid," the girl said, sniffing disdainfully. "Did you lose your class, moving out with the chickens and pigs?"

Helen frowned. "I suppose you would resist if Peter asked you to sit on a park bench with him? I can't remember you ever being such a goody-two-shoes."

"Wow!" the girl exclaimed, momentarily forgetting about the large "Quiet" sign over her head. "You must be getting goofy sitting out there on that farm. Goofy or just plain crude!"

The head librarian came to shush the girls, and Helen's former classmate turned to walk away from her. "Don't go!" Helen whispered sharply, catching her friend's arm. "We always got along so well. Why do you accuse me of bad taste and call me goofy because I let Peter kiss me? Is it just jealousy, or what?"

Her friend fixed Helen with a cold stare; then something within Helen's own eyes caused the girl to thaw just a bit. "Look, Helen," she began, "every girl daydreams once in a while, and I suppose we all tell fibs to our friends now and then, but I think it was in bad taste for you to say that Peter kissed you a couple of weeks ago. Say it was Bob, David, Hank; you know, anybody but Peter."

Helen shook her head. "It wasn't a fib. Peter did kiss me.

And what's wrong with Peter? You know he's the dreami-est boy in the class."

Tears began to form in her friend's eyes. "I don't know if you are serious or not," she told Helen. "If you're just being crude, then I really feel sorry for you, Helen." The girl took a deep breath, continued: "Peter *was* the dreami-est boy in our class. He was killed in an automobile acci-dent shortly after you moved away."

Helen could find no words to utter as she watched the back of her friend moving away from her. *Peter dead!* It simply could not be. She recognized another former class-mate across the library and nearly ran to the table where the girl sat flipping through a magazine. She confirmed the startling news of Peter's death.

Mrs. Helen Murad can provide no explanation of the experience which she had with an affectionate ghost nearly twenty years ago. But, she emphasizes, she knows that she sat on that park bench and received a warm kiss from a boy who had been dead for over a year, and she can offer the additional testimony of her mother, who saw Peter as unmistakably as Helen felt him.

Baron Roger de Rageot had two witnesses who clearly saw him with his phantom sweetheart. "Is it possible for three persons to share a hallucination? I think not," he writes in the July, 1967, issue of *Fate* magazine.

In the summer of 1965 Baron Rageot was called back to Paris to be at the bedside of his dying father. After his father had passed on, Rageot drifted to St. Tropez, Juan les Pins, Monte Carlo, Nice, Cannes, hoping to lose a mo-rose spirit among the gay crowds. At last he met Mireille in a little café, and soon the two of them were in love.

"She became my reason for existence," Rageot writes; "night and day I saw nothing but Mireille. We spent a de-licious summer and early fall in Paris."

They would have been married, but too soon, it seemed, Rageot's profession called him back to the United States.

He had been away for seven months on a leave of absence, and he could not dally any longer. For reasons which Rageot does not care to divulge to his readers, it was impossible for him to bring Mireille back to America with him at that time, and so they parted.

As they had promised, the two lovers exchanged letters constantly; then: ". . . abruptly and soon her letters ceased to come. This plunged me into another period of gloom."

Baron Rageot began spending long hours with his friends in a vain attempt to forget his sorrow and his depression. On December 21, 1965, he sat with two close friends discussing philosophy, his mind, as always, on Mireille. A knock sounded at his studio door, and when he bade the caller enter, he was astounded to see his darling Mireille suddenly standing before him.

Mireille was beautiful and serene, amused at his obvious state of surprise and confusion. Rageot remembers her black slacks, a sky-blue sweater which brought out the glow of her amber complexion, her gold high-heeled shoes, and, of course, her magnificent dark hair that fell about her shoulders.

The lovers rushed to each other's arms, embracing wildly, dancing madly about the room. His friends soon left them alone, after having been completely captivated by Mireille's charm and gentle personality.

"We talked endlessly," Baron Rageot tells us, "but each time I asked her how she came to my studio from Paris, or for details of her voyage, she would say, 'Hush now, be quiet. I am here, and that's all that's important.' "

When they went to bed that night, Rageot held his dear Mireille tightly, as if he were fearful that she might suddenly vanish. Once, much later in the night, he reached out for her and was reassured by her presence. She lay propped up on an elbow, her somber eyes gazing at him with love and kindness. When she asked him why he slept so restlessly, Rageot answered her frankly: "Because . . . I am afraid you are going to vanish, vaporize, disappear. I have that feeling."

Mireille laughed at his fears, told him to go back to sleep. Yet, when Rageot awakened the next morning, his love was gone.

"The bed where Mireille had slept was still warm; the pillow still held the shape of her dear head." But Mireille had vanished, leaving behind only one tangible bit of evidence that she had ever been there—"a music record of the famous singer Tino-Rossi, which she had given me, knowing my great fondness for the Corsican singer." They had played the record many times that night, and it still remained on the turntable of his phonograph.

Since that cold December dawn when Mireille disappeared, Baron Rageot has truly become a haunted lover. He has returned to Paris twice, visiting all their old haunts, talking to friends who had known of their love. From all he can learn, Mireille seems to have vanished from Paris shortly after he sailed for the United States in the fall of 1965, and Rageot can find no one who has seen her since.

Rageot writes that he still has the record, which proves nothing to anyone but himself; the testimonies of his two friends, who "saw her with their own eyes"; and the statement of his maintenance man, who "is certain he saw a dark-haired woman wearing a light-blue sweater" leave Rageot's apartment that morning. Mireille had brought no luggage with her on her alleged trip from Paris, so she could leave no bags behind to offer any clue to her disappearance. The phantom Mireille has left Rageot a lonely, troubled man, restlessly seeking the shadow of his love.

6. DREAMS TO WARN, DREAMS TO SHARE

Gloria F. could remember her dream in sharp detail the next morning when she awakened. Her boyfriend Roger had asked her to go riding with him across the Illinois state line into Indiana. As they drove along the h ghway, they had collided with another car, and both vehicles sustained great damage. Through drops of blood blurring her vision, Gloria had watched a plump woman with her arm bandaged and in a sling crawl out of the other car.

With the dream images firmly implanted in her mind, Gloria refused Roger's offer of an automobile ride on that beautiful Sunday afternoon. "Come on," he coaxed. "Let's buzz over to Hammond and see if Indiana is as pretty as Illinois is today."

Gloria shook her head, told Roger about the dream that she had had the night before. "Are you going to let a silly dream interfere with an outing on a day like today?" He laughed. "There won't be any wreck with old Steady Hand at the wheel. I'll even get you home early. Is it okay, Mrs. F.?" he asked Gloria's mother, who was sitting on the porch swing reading the Sunday paper.

"I think an automobile ride would be pleasant on such a nice day," she answered, looking up from the recipe she was studying on the women's page. "Why don't you kids run along?"

Reluctantly, Gloria followed the triumphantly grinning Roger to his car. "Well, you drive carefully, Roger!"

And Roger did drive carefully, a point he was to emphasize repeatedly, until, halfway between Gary and Hammond, Indiana, they crashed into another car.

Gloria's head went through the windshield, and she staggered from Roger's automobile, wiping the blood out of her eyes. Dimly, she saw the driver of the other car removing himself from behind the wheel with great effort. The driver's wife, a very plump woman, was tugging at him with one good arm. Her other arm was bandaged and in a sling.

"If only I had followed the warning in my dream instead of listening to Mom and Roger," Gloria kept saying to herself as she sat in the doctor's office, waiting to have her skull stitched closed.

Carla Patsuris' reputation for having prophetic dreams allowed her husband to quietly prepare for his death, even though she herself, as she reported her nocturnal premonitions, did not realize the bizarre pattern her dreams had been taking until after her husband's burial.

According to Mrs. Patsuris ("Dreaming the Future," *Fate*, February, 1957), one month after his death her husband appeared to her in a dream. As was her custom, the next morning she made note of the dream in her journal. "With the notebook open, I reread dreams from the past six months. I was amazed to discover I had been warned of Michael's death, even to the very day, yet had not been alert enough to realize I was being warned."

Mrs. Patsuris had dreamed that her husband would be struck down in the street by a car. Damages would be paid for the accident, but she, not her husband, would collect them.

Michael Patsuris was knocked down in the street and injured by a car on January 1, 1956. Mrs. Patsuris later collected a small sum of money after her husband's burial.

On January 17, 1956, she dreamed that she was frantically searching for her husband. She found, instead, a long black slip and a black dress. She put them on, and she awoke weeping.

On February 10 she dreamed that Michael had disappeared, taking with him only one suit and leaving behind everything else he owned. She called his business to inquire after him, and she was told that he was gone and would not return. Before she hung up, they reminded her that it was Michael's birthday. Again, she had awakened in tears.

On June 6 Mrs. Patsuris had another dream in which she was desperately searching for her husband. At last she saw him, standing across a river, speaking with her grandfather, who had died in 1924.

"I had told my husband about all of my dreams, and I believe he saw what I did not, for he had a lawyer draw up his will on June 21, 1956," Mrs. Patsuris wrote. "He died the next day, his birthday."

It would appear that Mrs. Patsuris' unconscious was steadily providing her with forewarnings of her husband's approaching death as she lay in the dream state. *First,* the preview of Michael's accident in the manner in which it occurred; *second,* the emotionality of dressing in black for Michael's funeral; *third,* a foreshadowing of the death date, Michael's birthday, and another preview of the funeral, *i.e.,* Michael taking only one suit, leaving everything else behind; *fourth,* the common symbol of death, "standing across a river."

"I was very much in love with a sailor stationed on the battleship USS *Oklahoma,*" Mrs. M. T. writes. "We wrote each other regularly, and he told me he only lived for the day when he could come home and marry me.

"On December 6, 1941, I received a letter from him in

which he told me of a terrible dream which he had had. He said that he had dreamed that he had been lying in his bunk and that he had heard me calling his name and weeping loudly. I sounded as though I was in deep pain and sorrow, and he tried to get up to help me, but he found that he could not move. He no longer seemed to have any control over his body. He felt tied down to his bunk with heavy, wet ropes. He couldn't even answer me, but just had to lie there in anguish and listen to me call his name and weep.

"I sat right down to write him a letter to tell him that I was fine and that he shouldn't worry about me. I never sent the letter. The next day was Sunday, December 7, and the *Oklahoma* went down in the attack on Pearl Harbor. I lay all night weeping and calling the name of my lost sailor."

The enigma of the precognitive dream has long fascinated mankind and has, from time to time, received scientific attention in "dream labs" established in various universities and hospitals.

It seems to this author that some level of the unconscious mind may well be aware of the future and that it may occasionally flash a dramatic bit or scene to the conscious mind in a dream or a trance, both of which are altered states of consciousness. Psychical researcher H. F. Saltmarsh theorized that what we with our conscious level of mind term the "present moment" is not a point of time, but a small time interval called the "specious present." According to Saltmarsh's theory, our unconscious minds may be able to encompass a larger "specious present" than our conscious level of being. If, on occasion, some of this unconscious knowledge were to burst into the conscious, it might be interpreted as either a memory of a past event or a precognition of a future event. We know that those events which we term our past are neatly cataloged somewhere in our unconscious. Some psychical researchers, such as Saltmarsh, believe that all events—past, present, and future

—are part of the "present," and Eternal Now, for the deeper, transcendental level of the unconscious.

The telepathic dream has recently received a great deal of attention through the scientific inquiry of the Dream Laboratory at the Maimonides Medical Center in Brooklyn, New York. The experiments undertaken by the Dream Lab were designed to test the hypothesis that the altered state of consciousness associated with dreaming favors the appearance in the dream of a telepathically received stimulus. Eight experimental studies conducted by the laboratory between 1964 and 1969 produced five studies with statistically significant results.

In addition to the formal experimental studies, a number of pilot sessions were undertaken with equally rigid precautions against any kind of sensory leakage. Between March 25, 1964, and December 19, 1969, eighty-three pilot sessions involving one or more agents [senders] and a single sleeping subject [receiver] had been completed by the Dream Lab.

In a report prepared for the 1970 meeting of the Association for the Psychophysiological Study of Sleep in Santa Fe, New Mexico, Montague Ullman, Stanley Krippner, and Charles Honorton of the Maimonides Medical Center state: "For these pilot sessions, judging of correspondences between the randomly selected target and dream content was accomplished by presenting outside judges with the entire target pool for that night and asking them to assign the rank of number one to that target picture which most closely resembled [the subject's] dreams and associational material. The other targets were also ranked on a similar basis. If the actual target was given a rank within the top half of the distribution (*e.g.*, number one or number two of a four-target pool), the rank was considered a 'hit,' supporting the telepathy hypothesis.

"For the eighty-three pilot telepathy sessions completed by the end of 1969, the judges assigned sixty-four 'hits' and nineteen 'misses.' This distribution is statistically significant. . . . Of these eighty-three sessions, eleven were held with a relative (father, mother, spouse, sibling) serving as [agent], rather than a Dream Laboratory staff member. For these sessions there are nine 'hits' and two 'misses.' "

The latter point is especially germane to a critical thesis of this book, *i.e.*, that paranormal phenomena function most efficiently and dramatically between agent and percipient who cherish strong emotional feelings toward one another.

Consider the telepathic dream experienced by Mrs. G. D. of Wyoming.

Due to severe drought conditions in the ranchlands, Mrs. G. D. had taken a job in town in order to help out financially. During the summer she had commuted, but in the winter, because of the bad weather and the poor roads, Mrs. G. D. rented a small house in town while her husband and two sons stayed at the ranch.

At 3:00 A.M. on a January morning, the woman awakened with the acrid odor of burning cloth offending her nostrils. Terrified by the thought that her house might be on fire, she got out of bed and checked the small home thoroughly. Although she found no fire in the house which she was renting, the feeling of danger persisted. She concluded that the fire must be in the home in which her husband and sons lay sleeping.

Mrs. G. D. called the ranch, but no one answered. She insisted that the operator keep trying. At last she heard the click of the receiver being lifted, and nearly simultaneously with his "hello," she heard her older son coughing.

"Are you all right, Billie?" she shouted into the receiver.

"Mom! Mom! The house is full of smoke!"

Mrs. G. D. told her boy not to panic. "Go wake up Daddy and Jimmy. Find out where the smoke is coming from, put out the fire, and call me back!"

After an excruciatingly long thirty minutes, Mr. D. called his wife. The boys had placed their gloves on the wood box to dry out that evening when they had come in from chores. Sometime during the night a spark had popped out of the stove and had landed on one of the gloves. The gloves had smoldered until they had burst into flame. When they located the fire, the gloves had been completely burned and the wood in the box was just beginning to crackle into flame.

Mrs. G. D. went back to bed, relieved that no real damage had been done to their ranchhome. "But I know that if I had not had that strange dream and smelled smoke where there was none and called the ranch, my home would have burned to the ground with my three loved ones in it," she stated in her account of the telepathic dream.

Sometimes, it appears, a telepathic bond between a man and a woman is so strong that they can share dreams. Numerous couples report having had common dreams or having been able to awake with an awareness of what the other had been experiencing in the dream state. Not long ago, a medium told this author of a dramatic dream in which he and his wife had interacted.

"My wife had gone to bed rather early that night, and she was already sound asleep when I decided to crawl beneath the covers. I doubt if I had been asleep more than a few moments when I became aware of my wife calling to me for help. Somehow I answered that call, and I crossed over into her dream.

"My wife was crouching in a dank cave, cowering before some hideous, beastlike creature. I was frightened when I saw the hulking monster slavering over Arlene, but a part of my mind reminded me that this was only a dream. So, with a courage found only in bottles and dreams, I charged the monster with both my fists flailing.

"It turned out to be a battle royal! I could feel my fists thud against his bulk, and his rough, scaly flesh soon made my knuckles bloody. And it landed some good ones on me, too. Once I felt its talons rip my cheek, and I know I must have cried out in pain. It seemed as though I might be winning, when I heard Arlene screaming behind me. I managed to look over my shoulder, and I was horrified to see that the damned thing had called reinforcements. One hideous brute was holding Arlene by the shoulders while another demon was ripping off her pajama bottoms. A quick glance at the creatures' lower bodies told me that they were emphatically male, and there was little question as to their designs on Arlene.

"Then—why I hadn't thought of it before I don't know —I called upon my spirit guide for some reinforcements of my own. Instantly, in answer to my mental summons, Brave Knife appeared with two other warriors, each of them brandishing heavy war clubs. The ensuing donnybrook would have done credit to any John Wayne western.

"After we had beaten off the grotesque 'bad guys,' I scooped the sobbing Arlene up in my arms. At that moment we awakened from our bizarre mutual dream.

"But the really eerie part is that we awakened in the middle of the bedroom with me holding Arlene just as I had been in the dream. Arlene's hair was disheveled, and the bottom of her pajamas were off. Arlene gasped and touched a finger gingerly to my cheek. Blood was trickling down over my chin from a deep scratch on my cheekbone. My pajamas were ripped in three places. And someone had turned all the bedroom lights on.

"Had we somehow made the dream become a pseudo-reality by acting out its weird and monstrous story line? Or had Arlene drawn us into a shadow world wherein grotesque night creatures dwell? I cannot really answer those questions, but I do know that in spite of strenuous housecleaning, the bottom half of Arlene's pajamas never have turned up."

Mrs. C. H. C. dreamed that she died, and it may have been only the intervention of her husband, who was having a similar dream, that prevented her dream from coming true.

"I dreamed that I had been shot by a thief as I walked on the street," Mrs. C. H. C. said in her account of the strange dream. "Police officers came running up, and they, in turn, shot the criminal, but all that was too late to do me any good. They stretched my body out on a park bench, and I suddenly found myself walking through unfamiliar hilly and barren country.

"I walked on and on, watching the light fade and the countryside grow darker. Deep blackness was closing in around me, when I heard my husband shouting in my ear: 'Honey! Honey! Don't leave me!' I heard his words over and over again, like a needle stuck in the groove of a phonograph record.

"I wanted to move, yet I could not. I wanted to answer him, but no sound came from my throat. I no longer had any control over my body. Dimly, I became aware of my husband sitting up in bed, turning me over on my back. I felt just a trickle of life returning to my body. I found myself awake, my sleeping husband bent over me. I managed to pat his hand, and he settled back down in bed with a deep sigh. Through all of his exertions, he had never awakened.

"I lay there for quite some time, cautiously trying all my loggy members to see if they were all working once again. At last I drifted back into an uneasy sleep.

"When the alarm went off that next morning, I awakened to find my husband holding me close to him. He told me that he had dreamed that I was leaving him forever to walk into a strange, barren land. He could not follow me past a barrier, but he could stand at the border and call for me to return."

Mrs. C. H. C. told her husband of her dream of death, and they lay there for several minutes marveling over the strange manner in which the dream states had been shared. Mr. C. raised himself on an elbow, started to speak, then stopped, a ghastly pallor draining his features of their normally ruddy hue. He reached to the bedside table and handed his wife a mirror.

"One look shocked me," Mrs. C. H. C. stated. "The skin under my eyes, around my mouth, and at the edge of my nostrils was blue. It felt cold and lifeless. My fingernails were blue, and so were my toenails and the palms of my hands. My whole body was still rather unmanageable. My husband noticed a place in my eye where the white seemed to have congealed.

"The blue left my fingernails and my palms, and I regained the use of my body after a few hours, but it took a week for the blue on my face to go away. I still have the spot in my eye. Once when a doctor saw it, he said that I must have been very close to death at some time for such a spot to have formed."

Dreams to warn, dreams to share, and a bit later, we shall examine the claims of men and women who boast dream lovers who came true. First, however, we shall have more to say about those individuals who accomplished telepathic link-ups by tuning each other in on their "mental radios."

7. LOVERS WHO TUNE IN
MENTAL RADIOS

We borrow our chapter title from the term which novelist Upton Sinclair coined for telepathic transmission and reception in the experiments which he conducted with his wife and his brother-in-law, R. I. Irwin. In 1930 Sinclair published the record of those experiments, in which Mrs. Sinclair had always served as the subject.

According to the novelist, the agent [when Irwin served as the agent, he "transmitted" from over forty miles away] would make a set of drawings of such simple items as a nest with eggs, a flower, a tree, and enclose each sketch in an opaque envelope. At the agreed-upon time, or later, Mrs. Sinclair would lie down on a couch and allow her mind and body to enter a state of total relaxation.

The subject soon learned that in order to achieve the best results in such tests, one must develop the ability to hold in consciousness, without any sense of strain, a single idea, such as the petal of a flower. Patterns of association must not be allowed to develop, and, above all, no thinking about the idea of telepathic transfer must take place. A completely relaxed state of body and mind must be accomplished.

In the experiments of the Sinclairs, it becomes difficult

to measure their actual success with the drawings, because often an idea associated with a sketch would come across rather than an explicit description of the sketch itself. In their own evaluation of the series of tests, the Sinclairs adjudged 65 successful "hits," 70 "misses," and 155 partial successes.

In this chapter we shall not be detailing the results of planned experiments in telepathy, but rather, the extraordinary experiences of men and women who were granted spontaneous demonstrations of the extrasensory transfer of mental stimuli.

Recently, David Hoy, the bearded, bespectacled, king-sized psychic, who continues to gain a vast following with his nightclub performances, lectures, and demonstrations of ESP for businessmen, told me a story of a telepathic transfer that, if heeded, could have saved a life and prevented a woman from becoming a truly haunted lover.

"Mariann is a famous songwriter, well known to composers and publishers on both coasts. She is also world-famous among musicians for the number of hits she has written. Mariann, who had written for Broadway as well as for major rock groups, had met and fallen in love with a musician named Roger. Since both Mariann and Roger were in the entertainment field, both traveled constantly. Their romantic interludes were forced to be brief, and their telephone bills totaled to staggering amounts.

"During the course of their romance, they both became interested in telepathy, and they often attempted long-distance tests of communication.

"One evening while Roger was in New York and Mariann was in Los Angeles, she felt a sense of dread that, in her mind, she knew was connected with her lover. She placed a call to his hotel room in New York and told him of her strong impression of danger.

"Roger laughed it off. 'Don't worry about it, darling. I love you, and the only thing wrong with me is that I am so tired. My bones ache from standing so long; my lips hurt from blowing that horn; and my heart aches because I am away from you.'

"Mariann persisted that her telepathic impression of danger was strong. Roger ignored her warnings, mumbled on in a sleepy voice about his love for her. Then Mariann no longer got a response from the exhausted Roger. He had fallen asleep. She called loudly over the receiver, but she could not awaken him. The feeling of dread was getting stronger. Mariann knew that Roger was in great danger, but since he had not hung up his receiver, she was unable to get a disconnect on her own line so she could redial the hotel desk.

"Before long Mariann was in a panic. She quickly dressed and went to a nearby phone and called Roger's hotel. They told her, of course, that his line was busy. It was only after much pleading on Mariann's part that the manager agreed to make a check of Roger's room. She held the line open while a bellhop was sent to investigate.

"A few moments later, Mariann was told that her husband-to-be had been found dead.

"As the authorities later reconstructed the story, Roger had fallen asleep smoking in bed while Mariann had still been talking to him. The bedclothes had immediately caught fire, and Roger had suffocated from the dense smoke.

"While Roger lay holding the receiver only inches from his ear, he had failed to respond to the cries of his lover, who, through telepathy, had been warned that his life was in danger."

On July 2, 1951, the Los Angeles *Daily Mirror* published an account of the accidental drowning of Thomas Wall. The twenty-five-year-old man had drowned in Mac-Arthur Park Lake while scores of spectators had watched helplessly from the shore, less than two hundred feet away. His companion, Joseph Cefalu, managed to swim to shore after making a futile attempt to save Wall.

Frances Wall, the dead man's wife, arrived on the scene shortly after the body was recovered. A premonition that something had happened to Wall had brought her from home.

William H. Gilroy investigated the incident and obtained statements from Joseph Cefalu and Frances Wall. According to Cefalu, Tom Wall had stopped by his apartment and asked him to go to the park with him. They took a sunbath, then, at Wall's suggestion, rented a canoe. They had started across the lake when Wall suddenly became concerned about the time. He had promised his wife that he would take her to dinner and a show that night. For some reason, Cefalu stated, Wall had stood up in the canoe and they had capsized.

In Frances Wall's account, she told how she had declined Tom's suggestion to go to the park and sunbathe. During the early afternoon she had worked about the house, bathed, put her hair up in curlers. She lay down to read, dozed off; then she was wide awake, hearing her husband's voice crying: "Frances, come to the park! I'm drowning!"

"His voice was as loud and distinct as though he were right in the room with me," she told Gilroy. "I sat there stunned and sick. Again his voice cried out, 'Frances, Frances, please hurry.' I don't remember how or what I put on, but I found myself outside the apartment, running toward the park. Before I had traveled half the distance to the lake, I saw a crowd gathering near the shore, and I knew without going nearer that my Tommy had gone away from me forever.

"Much later someone found me wandering about the streets and brought me home."

When Mrs. E. S. V. experienced extreme feelings of uneasiness and nausea, she somehow knew that the sensations were related to her husband.

"Tony was at work," she said. "Although he had looked

well when he left for his job, I knew that he was sick. It was as if I could actually hear him saying, 'Eleanor, please come and get me. I'm terribly sick.' And then waves of nausea would hit me."

Mrs. E. S. V. reached the point where she could no longer bear her uneasiness, and she changed her dress and drove to the factory where her husband worked. An inquiry at the desk produced the information that Mr. V. was not at his job, but was in the dispensary. The nurse there had been trying to call Mrs. V. at home, but had not received an answer.

When Mrs. E. S. V. walked into the dispensary, she found her husband sitting down, extremely pale, and in great pain. Two of his co-workers, who had helped him into the office, stood on either side, ready to assist again if need be. Mrs. E. S. V. accepted their offer to help her husband into her car.

"What made you come after me?" her husband asked, once she had him home and in bed.

"I don't really know," she admitted. "I felt I was just being silly, but I had a terrible feeling of uneasiness that you were sick and in pain."

"Well, you were right," he sighed. "You came just when I needed you. You amazed everyone when you came walking into the dispensary while the nurse was trying to call you at home."

A psychic sensitive told this author of the time that she rejected a telepathic marriage proposal.

"I was just seventeen, and my mediumistic abilities were developing rapidly," the woman, whom we shall call Salena, said. "An older Spiritualist minister, who had already gone through three wives, decided that I should marry him and he would really develop me into a powerful medium. The fact that I considered him old enough to be my grandfather did not seem to concern him at all.

"One night as I was just drifting off to sleep, I became

aware of a presence in my bedroom. Although I could see no one, I could clearly hear the sound of this man's voice pleading with me to marry him. I laughed. Did he really think that such a novel method of proposing would melt my cold, cold heart?

" 'Listen, you old stick,' I thought with all my being, 'as far as I'm concerned, if you were the last man on earth, you would still have to live alone!'

"The next day the minister came around to our house and lectured both me and my mother about what a rude young lady I was. I told him that I had no idea what he was talking about, that I had my entire family as witnesses to the fact that I had gone to bed early that night. 'If you came around here, Reverend,' I said in wide-eyed innocence, 'I certainly didn't see you.'

" 'But you *heard* me,' he said, as he walked away grumbling, 'and neither of us needs any witnesses to know what we are talking about.' "

A student in an Eastern college, to whom we shall give the pseudonym Edgar Morris, found out that it is possible to hurt the ones we love telepathically, as well as emotionally.

Edgar had always been a high academic achiever, and by the time he was a sophomore, the word was out that if one were in a class with Edgar, he was the one who would raise the class curve on examinations. For those students who were also intensely academically oriented, Edgar Morris became *the* man to beat. Then, near the close of his sophomore year, Edgar met Alice, and Cupid's deadly darts began to take their toll of his study time.

"The climax came after this big test in sociology," Edgar said. "When the grades were posted, I was shocked to see that I had barely received a passing mark. Some of the fellows in the class cheered, and nearly everyone was laughing at my humiliation. One of my rivals in the class passed me in the corridor and whispered: 'Every Samson has his Delilah!' "

Edgar Morris was not so academically aloof that he could not feel the pinch of terrible pride. He went to a campus coffee house with his closest friend and told him of his intention of breaking off with Alice. "Hey, c'mon, man. You're throwing away a great chick like Alice because of a nick in your grades? You're unreal, baby," his friend said, shaking his head sadly.

"I'm serious," Edgar replied. "I cannot jeopardize my academic standing. Perhaps later we might be able to take up again. I hereby decree that as of this afternoon, at 3:55 P.M., Alice and I are no longer a thing."

Edgar bade his friend farewell and went back to his room to attack the books. Perhaps it was not too late to regain the precious points which he had lost in his sociology class.

After two days had passed, Edgar began to notice that he had not seen Alice in the coffee house or in the one class they shared. When he inquired about her, he learned from one of her friends that Alice lay in a strange semicoma at the campus health service. According to her friend, Alice had been perfectly well until about four o'clock two days before. At that time, she had suddenly heaved a deep sigh and fainted. Neither the girls nor the campus doctor had been able to revive Alice for more than short periods of consciousness.

Edgar went directly to the health service and asked to see Alice. Although she seemed to be lying on her bed in a light trance state, she became immediately animated the moment Edgar walked into the room. "You deceitful creep!" she screamed. "So I no longer mean anything to you! So you are going to leave me! You cruel . . . cruel . . ."

"For a second there," Edgar said, "Alice couldn't think of a word, and I couldn't think of anything to do. Then I walked over to her bed and kissed her and told her that she was all upset over nothing. Alice was out of the infirmary in a couple of days, and since that time, I have been finding ways to budget my time so that neither Alice nor my studies are neglected."

Many of us have known couples who have grown so close over the years that it is difficult to visualize one of them without the other. It may well be that such couples form an enormously powerful telepathic bond which is responsible for those cases where we read that an elderly man has passed away, only to be followed in death a few days later by his mate. Not long ago this author received an account where such a telepathic link-up may have been involved in the near-death of an elderly woman.

"Russell C. had always been a powerful man," Mrs. R. S. said, "strong of body, mind, and will. Although theirs had been a happy marriage, Anna C. had often been forced to bend to the desires of her indomitable husband. At last, when he was nearly eighty, his powerful old frame began to weaken, and Russell was forced to become a virtual invalid. His fierce pride suffered, as he had never been ill a day in his life. His humiliation was all the greater because Anna, who had always been such a frail little woman, remained active and well.

"Russell was, at last, taken to a hospital. His doctor realized that the old man was still dictating to his wife, and she was dutifully waiting on him hand and foot. Russell had been in the hospital about a week, when, one night, I stopped by to visit Anna.

"She had excused herself to put the coffeepot on, when she clutched for her throat and buckled at the knees. I ran to her side, fearing that she had suffered a stroke. She was pale and weak, and I could find no pulse. I grabbed the telephone and dialed her doctor. When there was no answer, I tried to remain calm. Anna's color seemed to be returning, and encouraged by this sign, I began gently patting and rubbing her arms.

"In a few moments she opened her eyes and began **to**

apologize for the funny feeling that had come over her. Her voice was thin and weak, but she insisted that she was all right. I helped her to a chair, while she kept apologizing for her unseemly behavior.

"At this point the telephone rang. I took the call while Anna sat weakly in her chair. It was her husband's doctor. Russell had taken a turn for the worse about an hour before. According to the doctor, the old man had seemed to be pulling out of it, but then he seemed to relinquish his hold on life. The physician recommended that Anna get to the hospital as soon as possible.

"Russell died that night. Although her doctor was unable to find any cause for Anna's sudden seizure, I will always wonder if that strong-willed, possessive husband had not intended to take his beloved wife along with him."

In the case of Mrs. M. W., a telepathic call from her husband's hospital bed drove her to accomplish the action necessary to save his life.

"Rick had come down with a bad case of influenza," she said in her account of the experience, "and I was staying at home with our children while he received medical attention in the hospital. I had just started to drift off that night when I clearly heard Rick's voice calling to me: 'Honey, I'm dying. Help me! Help me! I'm dying, but no one knows it!' "

Mrs. M. W. did not hesitate to act. She saw no need to attempt a rationalization of the voice. She knew that she had not been dreaming, and she knew that she had heard her husband's voice.

"It was after midnight when I arrived at the hospital, and, of course, I was coldly informed that visiting hours were over. I insisted that they examine my husband. Again, in a crisp, antiseptic manner, I was told that a night nurse had just looked in on my husband and that he was sleeping restfully.

"I could not be put off. I insisted that they call a doctor

to examine him or I would run into that room and look at him myself. I am not a small woman, and they could see that I meant what I said. They summoned a doctor, who listened wearily to their story and my pleas; then, in order to humor me, he agreed to look in on my husband.

"I waited at the desk a few moments, then brushed aside a nurse to run up the stairs which led to my husband's corridor. 'Good lord!' I heard the doctor's harsh whisper. 'This man is dying!' "

Quick work on the part of the doctor and the nurses saved Rick W.'s life. Later, when he had regained consciousness, he told his wife how he had lain there, knowing he was dying, and how he had desperately sought to send a cry for help to her at home. His conviction that his thoughts could make his wife act had saved his life.

In the December, 1954, issue of *Fate* magazine, Charlotte T. Mazue of Los Angeles, California, wrote of how she telepathically directed her husband to a new apartment which he had never seen.

The incident occurred during the war year of 1942. Mrs. Mazue moved from Huntington Park to a choice apartment in Hollywood when her husband, Charles, was stationed temporarily near San Francisco. She thought of how happy her husband would be with the new apartment, but about 2:30 one afternoon, she got the distinct feeling that Charles was trying to reach her telepathically. Perhaps Charles had acquired a leave. This thought filled her with concern as well as joyful anticipation, for she had not yet written to Charles to inform him of the new address.

"I quietly repeated to myself every hour before retiring, 'Honey, we now live in Hollywood. Come to Kingsley Drive at Santa Monica Boulevard. Rear of gift shop. Redbrick court. Upstairs at the back,' " Mrs. Mazue wrote.

It started to rain when she retired at 10:30 P.M. At half-past midnight, the door chimes brought her tumbling out of bed, calling: "Coming, dear!" She confidently opened the door to find a drenched, but smiling, Charles. "So this is home," he said, as he hugged her close to him.

Charles told her later that he, of course, had had no idea that she had moved. "Seems as if someone pushed and pulled me here. I hitchhiked in and told the driver to let me out at Kingsley Drive and Santa Monica Boulevard. Then I walked to the rear of the gift shop and upstairs to you. Funny thing is, I distinctly heard you say, 'That's right, darling.' "

Experimental psychologist Dr. Stanley Krippner is one of those researchers who feel that the scientific establishment will eventually have to revise its image of man on the basis of telepathic evidence. At present, Dr. Krippner observes, psychology and psychiatry view each person as an entity separated from everyone else, as an alienated being.

"Telepathy may teach us that in the basic fabric of life everything and everyone is linked, that man is continuously enmeshed, that he is always an integral part of all life on the face of the earth," Dr. Krippner says. "So far the scientific establishment has ignored this possibility; it will, for one thing, refute many of their basic concepts."

Regardless of the opposing dicta of scientific orthodoxy which decree that such mental transmissions and receptions are "impossible," there are thousands of men and women who have discovered through some dramatic telepathic link-up that their lives are, indeed, "continuously enmeshed."

8. SEXUAL MOLESTERS
FROM THE SPIRIT WORLD

In desperation, a thirty-nine-year-old widow in Pretoria, South Africa, appealed to the city council for new housing after repeated unwelcome advances from a spirit lover that had made her house its home. Anna De La Ravera told newsmen that she and her children had noticed an eerie quality to the house shortly after they had moved in, in November of 1967. Mrs. De La Ravera said that she had found mysterious crosses chalked on the doors and a piece of pork on a nail in the master bedroom.

In March, 1968, Mrs. De La Ravera returned home one day to find a man dressed in gray sitting on the front porch. "What do you want?" she demanded. In response to her query, the man stood up and walked into the house through the closed and locked front door.

Although Mrs. De La Ravera could discover no trace of the phantom when she unlocked her door, he materialized that night in her bedroom and tried to pull the covers off her bed. The spirit wanted to make love, but Mrs. De La Ravera was having none of his persistent desires. According to the beleaguered widow, her unwelcome lover was covered with long hair and had long, curved fingernails.

The passionate phantom relentlessly continued his amorous advances in the weeks that followed, until Mrs. De La Ravera could no longer tolerate another night in the accursed house.

"My two sons, aged nine and twelve, have seen nothing," she said in her appeal to the Pretoria City Council, "but my three-year-old daughter has cried, 'Mama, I'm scared. He'll bite me!'

"I have kept the lights on at night, but this does not seem to discourage the ghost. Once he switched off the lights and whispered to me, 'Be careful, I'm going to murder you!' "

The Pretoria City Council responded to the tormented widow's plight by assisting her in finding new housing. Once Mrs. De La Ravera had moved away from the diseased home which harbored the demanding sexual molester from the spirit world, she was able to spend her nights undisturbed by ethereal gropings.

About two years ago, at eleven o'clock one night, a Wisconsin co-ed was lying in her bed, drifting off to sleep. With some irritation, she became aware that something was pulling at her bedclothes, then tugging at her leg. She opened her eyes to see a hideous, hairy creature, grinning lustfully at her and pulling her slowly across the bed.

"I was paralyzed," she told one of this author's correspondents. "I could neither move nor cry out. There was no mistaking what plans the grotesque male creature had in mind for me. Then I thought very intensely, 'God save me!' There was a very brilliant flash of light at the ceiling, and the creature disappeared. I wore a cross for a long time after that."

Another young woman reports that she was falling asleep with a book in her hand one night when she felt someone or something enter her room.

"Whatever it was," she said, "it picked me up and tossed me in the air. I landed on the opposite side of the bed from the one I had been lying on. The door to the bathroom slammed shut, and I lay on the bed physically and emotionally drained. I lay there a long time before I had enough strength to get up. I was very frightened."

A young career woman from San Diego, California, writes that one night immediately after she had turned off her bedlamp, she heard a buzzing sound around her head.

"It moved in circles, and I can only describe it as a bee buzzing. Then it seemed to have a man's voice, and it kept buzzing over and over, 'I love you! I love you!'

"Whenever I turned the light on, it would go away. The second I snapped the lamp off, it would be back buzzing around my head.

"A few nights later, I had the sensation of someone getting into bed with me, and I heard the sound of breathing beside me. It smelled like rotton seaweed, and I was so frightened that I could not move. The next day the bed was wet on that side."

Mrs. N. S. is often required to travel away from home in her job with the state board of health. One night she lay in a clean motel room, dozing contentedly, when she felt someone get into bed with her.

"I was in light sleep," she stated in her account of the incident. "I forgot where I was for a moment and thought that I was at home and my husband was crawling in beside me. Then I suddenly remembered my strange surroundings. I jumped from the bed and turned on the light. I was prepared to emit a scream that would have brought the National Guard down on whoever had slipped into my bed, but the sounds died in my throat. There was no one in my bed. I was quite alone."

Mrs. N. S. went to the bathroom, got a drink of water, decided that she had dreamed the whole thing. She chuckled softly to herself, thought about what a story it would be to tell her husband, then fell instantly asleep.

"When I awoke the next morning," Mrs. N. S. said, "I stretched contentedly until, to my surprise and horror, I realized that a body was pressed full-length against mine. I lay shocked, frozen into immobility. Whoever lay beside me turned over, sighed noisily, and pressed a thigh familiarly against my own. I heard a male voice, muffled in the covers, say, 'Oh, how tiresome it gets traveling around the country.'

"At last panic grabbed me. I leaped from the bed and grabbed for a chair, which I would willingly have smashed against any intruder—if any intruder would have been there. Once again my bed was empty, but this time the pillow next to mine clearly showed the indentation of a head resting on it!"

Mrs. N. S. testified that although she usually likes to take her time getting dressed in the morning, she left that motel room in record speed.

A young woman from Oklahoma told another of this author's correspondents that it is her habit to take a hot bath immediately upon returning from work, then loll about a few moments in the nude, usually reading on her bed. One night she lay on her stomach doing her nails, with her feet sticking out over the foot of the bed. She had lain there for several minutes when she felt someone grab her by the ankles and turn her over on her back.

"Something invisible, yet of great strength, was seeking to spread my legs apart," she said. "I fought against this with all my will. The struggle must have gone on for several minutes. Every muscle in my thighs was screaming with pain of the constant tension, yet I would not yield and allow my genitals to be exposed in such a vulnerable manner.

"At last the pressure ceased, and I lay gasping on the bed. My nail polish had spilled, and the bedspread was stained. I had no time to worry about the mess, however. The foot of the mattress went down, as it does when a person sits on it. Still, I could see no one. The end of the bed went up again, and footsteps sounded walking to the head of the bed. My heart was thudding so hard in my chest that I could hardly breathe.

"The footsteps stopped at the head of the bed, and I looked up to see the figure of a man standing there. His face looked like a zombie's, like someone who has been dead for a long time.

"I couldn't make a sound, not even a squeak. Then the hideous thing smiled and reached out a hand as if to touch me. It was changing its tactics. From attempted rape to a smile. It was grotesque, but there was something about its eyes that seemed to make me want to stop resisting it. At last I found my voice and screamed at it to get out of my room. Thank God it disappeared, and it has never returned."

The mythos of the demon lover ("incubi" pester women; "succubi" seduce men) which leaves its ethereal habitat to venture out on lusty nocturnal forays in search of acquiescent human flesh is one that can be traced back to ancient times and whose strains can be found in all cultures. As the reader has just witnessed, such claims of supernatural sexual molesters cannot be relegated to a less sophisticated past. According to a good many men and women, who swear that they have encountered such sexual offenders from the spirit world, the demon lover is as much a bedroom nuisance in the twilight world of our supermarket-and-space-age culture as it was a bedchamber violator in the superstition-saturated and sexually tortured Middle Ages.

This author received a report not long ago of a "haunted house" which has within its walls a room wherein whoever has the courage to sleep on its canopied bed is beset with the most dreadful nightmares of suffocation and sexual assault. Screams have been heard echoing eerily down the corridors, and the evidence seems to indicate a point of emanation from somewhere within the psychically diseased room. According to tradition, a young woman was raped and murdered in that room, and the terrible emotion of that crime against her person has in some way penetrated the etheric atmosphere and almost attained a life of its own.

In the March, 1969, issue of *Fate,* Comtesse Madeleine de La Riviere told of how she and a companion had encountered such a tainted room in a Tyrolian castle when they were schoolgirls.

It was a room in a high tower, and its walls seemed covered with the stains of blood that had been spilled long ago. Two high, arched windows and a large, gaping opening were all that time had left of a balcony. Far below them, they could hear the roar of the river.

"There was an eerie horror, a smell of death, an aura of destruction in this empty tower," the Comtesse writes. Liesl, her companion, announced her intention of looking down at the river from the window. "As we stepped forward," she goes on, "it felt like wading through waist-high mud. It was like the nightmares in which you struggle with all your might to run but are paralyzed. . . ."

Then, as they reached the center of the room, they were no longer struggling to advance toward the window, they were being pushed! The Comtesse remembers clinging desperately to the stone of the windowsill. Liesl was closer to the outer part of the balcony, her body shaking, her face pale.

They knew that they must not think of falling, yet they began to laugh hysterically, as if plummeting to the roaring river below would be the most happy of experiences. "Did I hear *something else* laughing, too?" the Comtesse wonders. In desperation, Liesl called on the name of Jesus, and, suddenly, the awful spell was broken. They shook off their fear. Nothing held them anymore. They ran from the room, the tower, the castle, back to the school, where they arrived "feverish, sobbing, talking nonsense," and were put to bed by the schoolmistress.

Later they sought out the grizzled old gardener, who

told them the legend of the ghost of the wicked Count that haunted the castle. According to the old rustic, Count Wolfgang had been the worst of the robber barons. He took delight in torturing his victims in the tower room that was still stained with their blood. It was said that he had sold his soul to the devil, and the archfiend kept him from enemy's harm or Emperor's justice. He took luckless maidens from the villages, used them until he grew tired of them, then threw them from the tower balcony.

Count Wolfgang could not resist kidnapping a beautiful novice from a convent. The idea of violating a future bride of the Lord appealed to his satanic lust. The novice Lucia pushed aside the two servants who held her for their master's sexual demands and walked to the balcony's edge. Announcing that she chose death's embrace before that of the Count's, she crossed herself and stepped off the edge.

According to legend, "A gentle breeze lifted her up . . . with her veil and robes billowing. Lightly, easily as a feather, she floated down, taking no harm, and was deposited on firm ground safely outside the grim castle, where she sank down in grateful prayer."

That night the devil claimed Count Wolfgang's soul, the old gardener told the two girls, and from that time forth, the castle had been accursed with the fear and pain of the Count's victims. "And the Count's evil spirit still seeks to perform the awful deeds he committed while he lived," the old man declared. Liesl had saved them from the powers of darkness when she called upon the name of Jesus.

Count Wolfgang's malignant spirit is representative of a most deadly category of demon lovers. He is not really in the incubi class of entities, for his essence of evil sought to kill rather than to possess his victims sexually.

"I had a spirit lover when I was much younger," a female medium told this author in confidence, "and I wish that I had never allowed it to come into me. You see, I can no longer be satisfied by a mortal man. Sexual intercourse with my spirit lover was beyond description. I have never achieved such orgasms with any man in the flesh. When I got married, you know, I was disappointed. I tried not to blame my husband, but he just couldn't compare.

"You see, my spirit lover's penis could expand and enlarge itself until it filled my entire vagina, almost to the point of pain. But, oh, what pain, what delicious pain! And the act of intercourse could continue until I had come and come and was sexually satisfied to the point of exhaustion. With a mortal man, a woman gets one, maybe two or three chances a night to come. If the man comes fast or is tired, you're out of luck. It's not that way at all with a spirit lover. He just keeps on and on until you're completely satisfied.

"But my advice to any young female medium is not to get started sexually with any spirit. It'll ruin your chance for happiness with any man on the earth plane. A spirit lover might be able to screw like Pan himself, but he can't keep you warm on cold nights or buy your groceries. It's a terrible thing to judge a man while he's making love to you, but that is what will happen if you've had a spirit lover; and your man will be able to tell by the way you respond that he's way behind in the comparison. So I repeat, don't start with a spirit lover, or you might find yourself awfully lonely in your old age."

Another female medium allowed that a pesky spirit lover had tried to annoy her on a number of occasions. "I didn't go for that kind of thing at all," she said. "Whenever he would come around, I would turn him away with this benediction: 'God bless you and go back where you come from. You aren't welcome here!' "

An occultist who teaches a class in psychic development told this author that she always warns her students that their initial attempts at opening their unconscious minds could make them easy targets for such manifestations as the incubus and succubus.

"Too many of them don't realize what they're getting into when they undertake psychic development," she said, "so I must keep emphasizing that they are easy prey for a sexual molester from the other planes. Until they develop enough psychic strength and knowledge, their wide-open psyches can draw horny entities like a hound to bitch scent!

"Some students would be horrified if an entity jumped into bed with them. Others would like it too damn well. I must teach them to exercise control or, hell, marriage as an institution would disappear! There's always an entity hovering about who is all too willing to take care of anyone's sexual frustration."

Tarot reader Ron Warmoth told me of one of his clients who was being sexually molested at night by an unwelcome entity. "I tried to tell her that I would give her some rituals which would ward off the horny little devil, but I guess she had seen too many Dracula movies. She told me that she was going to bed that night wearing a sprig of garlic over her genitals.

"She was too embarrassed to tell me, but one of her closest friends told me that she had had to see her doctor the next day to have the garlic removed from deep inside her vagina, where her spirit lover had rammed it."

An occultist told this author of the time when she had been performing her yoga exercises in the nude and a large snake suddenly materialized and slithered up her exposed vagina. "It took every ounce of my strength and will to grab hold of that serpent's tail and pull it out of my genitals," she said, unable to suppress a shudder as the memory of the experience came back to her. "As soon as I had extracted it, it disappeared."

The next night when she did her exercises, she left her panties on, and although the large serpent did materialize again, it could do nothing but rise up and sway back and forth hypnotically. "But it couldn't hypnotize me into taking off my panties," the occultist said.

"Finally, after several nights of this, I expressed a wish that I might see who or what was doing this thing to me. That night when the serpent materialized, it dissolved into the image of a master. Perhaps my wish granted him the power to appear as other than a serpent. At least as a master he never molested me sexually. I know that in occult terms the serpent is the symbol of wisdom, but I know my Freud, too, and I can say that that serpent was one phallic symbol that really acted the part!"

If female occultists and mediums have confessed to both forced and reciprocal sexual liaisons with incubi, certain of their male counterparts have freely admitted physical dalliance with succubi.

"Them's fighting words if you refer to Bright Star as a succubus," a male medium growled when I asked him about sex in the spirit world. "Bright Star is my spirit guide. You've seen that television show where that Air Force fellow has the pretty genie in the jug? Well, my relationship with Bright Star is like that, only we take up where the television people clean it up for the kiddies.

"There is absolutely nothing immoral about our relationship, though," he was quick to point out. "Bright Star and I fell in love over a period of several years. We were married by a minister who is in spirit, and I have not known a woman of the earth plane since we were wed. I find that our new relationship has accelerated my powers as a medium."

A male witch told me how he had deliberately set about conjuring up a succubus. "I thought how groovy it would be if I could have a luscious spirit chick whenever I wanted her. No fuss, no muss, like with a flesh-and-blood chick. I wouldn't really have to get involved with a spirit doll."

He entered into an exhaustive regimen of incantation and conjuration and claims that he succeeded in summoning a succubus that looked like "Raquel Welch's big sister."

"Man, she would come some nights when I went through the rituals, and we would make it like you would not believe," he said. "She was nearly fifteen hundred years old, and she had learned every trick in the books. Maybe her body was kind of cold to the touch, but when I penetrated her vagina, it was like sticking my tool into molten lava."

Things ended rather badly for the witch and his cosmic concubine. He decided to go a bit kinky and set up some mirrors so he could have the added sensual pleasure of watching their myriad positions of love reflected again and again. What he saw in the mirror that night nearly caused him to lose his mind.

"Gawd," he moaned, clenching his teeth. "I still nearly puke whenever I think of it. I was making it with the most god-awful kind of reptilian creature right out of a wino's nightmare. And if it had taken me a long time to summon the beast, you will never guess what I went through getting rid of that toad woman!"

"So many of the young women who have experiences with incubi only report having some invisible thing make love to them or try to make love to them," a female medium told this author. "I'm not talking about witches, mediums, and occultists now," she emphasized, "but the college girls, career girls, young housewives, and teen-agers, who maybe suffer one or two assaults from an incubus. Sexual frustration seems to attract these creatures, these entities, and although they may feel like a human male to these girls, if they could view them—which, thank God, they usually cannot—they would see the most grotesque kind of animallike entities right out of some medieval painting of demons."

Continuing with her impromptu lecture, the medium said, "The incubi can come in several different forms—as an invisible entity; as an image of a loved one, either living or in spirit; as an image of an idealized love partner; or as a hideous gargoylelike beast. They attack the most vulnerable—the lonely, the frustrated, the unloved, the young who are unsure of their sex appeal. A young woman who lies in her bed at night, tossing, turning, longing for a lover in her arms, sends out vibrations that bring these entities from every dark corner in the etheric worlds."

Indiscriminate use of the Ouija board seems to be an almost sure-fire method of producing, if not a lusty spirit lover, a foul-talking, sex-obsessed spook that makes a passion of obscenity. Ed Wilcox interviewed showgirl Joan Myers [New York *Sunday News,* January 5, 1969] in regard to a hot-blooded spook that she claimed had been annoying her for three years.

The spirit, "Al," was after her "hot and heavy before her marriage," Wilcox reported, "and still hasn't let up one bit. . . . Sometimes his moods are soft and sweet in getting down to the nitty-gritty, and other times he sweeps convention aside and uses shocking language to express his dishonorable intentions."

Joan Myers clarified one point: "Al" had never been able to get off the Ouija board with his approach and do anything physical to her. "Al" first appeared one evening three years ago when another showgirl asked Joan to work the Ouija board with her in an attempt to contact her recently departed husband. The girl's husband came through, according to Joan, with many messages pertaining to important papers and unfinished business. Then "Al" butted into the conversation and hogged the board for the rest of the evening.

"Since then I guess I have played the board one hundred times or more," Joan Myers said. "I nearly always wind up with Al monopolizing the evening, telling me that he is crazy about me and sometimes using very explicit four-letter words to express his feelings and thoughts. Of course, I scold him when he talks dirty."

Although Joan has never been able to learn very much about "Al's" past life on earth, she says that the spirit predicted the date of her grandfather's death and the initials of her future husband. "I don't think Al likes the idea of my being married," the attractive blond showgirl said, "but there's not a hell of a lot he can do about it except say insulting things."

And one never knows to what lengths these sexual molesters from the spirit world might go to perform an insulting act. Not even the phenomenon of psychic photography remains free from the machinations of sexually obsessed incubi and succubi.

A former Spiritualist minister told this author of an experiment in psychic photography which she conducted with three rather prissy middle-aged women.

"When we developed the plate to see what the gentle spirits had brought us," she said, "we found that we had a picture of a huge, hairy penis!"

In my *Sex and the Supernatural,* an earlier work, this author wondered if the demon lover might not be a self-directed, psychokinetically projected personification of that dark, inaccessible part of the psyche in which resides the center of primitive instincts and the drive for sexual gratification. The "spirit lover" might cater to a particular psychic need brought about by the sexual frustration of the selfish, the self-centered, the narcissistic, who, because of their inner-directedness, fail to make a satisfactory sexual adjustment with a living love object and may even prefer to fantasize a sex partner while masturbating. But whether one looks to sexual psychopathology to explain the incubi and the succubi or to the darker regions of the unknown, wherein lie demons panting for human flesh, the phenomena of spirit lovers present dramatic instances in which the powerful emotions and the vibrant life force of man can produce "haunted lovers."

9. OTHER-WORLDLY LOVERS FROM UFOs

The letters have a monotonous sameness about them, yet they contain a strong note of urgency, and they come from all sections of the country and overseas.

"Dear Mr. Steiger," a typical letter begins, "I am not a nut; I am on the dean's list at————College, majoring in physics. This is my real name, and if you are suspicious of me, you can check me out. Last summer I saw a flying saucer at close range. It hovered over my car for several miles as I drove to my parents' farm home. It was definitely a metallic object. Shortly after that sighting, I was aware of something in my bedroom one night as I was preparing for bed. I could see nothing, but I could not shake a feeling of uneasiness. . . . I was not yet asleep when I felt a pressure on the bed beside me. When I sat up, I saw nothing, but I felt *something* fondling my breasts. I wanted to scream, to get out of bed, but I was unable to move. . . . I remember nothing more until I awakened the next morning, but I have reason to believe that something made love to me while I slept. I believe this incident was associated in some way with my sighting the UFO."

A series of letters from a college girl in a Northwestern state detailed how an invisible *something* began to annoy her in her bedroom after her sighting of UFO. She described fainting spells and inertia which would come over her whenever she attempted to tell anyone of her experiences. Once, she said, she had fainted twice while writing to this author, because *they* were interfering, censoring her thoughts.

In one of her letters she writes: "I felt something heavy at the foot of my bed. It moved to the far left. Then I felt nothing. A few seconds later I felt a warm radiation just to the left of where I was lying, so I moved to the far right of the bed. The heat began to radiate warmer and warmer, until I was sweating. I threw off the covers until it cooled off. Then after I was lying down again, it started to get warmer. This continued all through the night."

This young co-ed, who planned a career in law enforcement, continued to write to this author, describing continued materializations and testifying that "aliens" walked among us, infiltrating our society on all levels. "You can tell them by their eyes," she wrote, just before I received a farewell letter saying that "they" no longer wished her to write to me. "I have come to realize that they are here to help us, and we should cooperate with them."

An extremely lengthy letter from a young female chemist told of her sexual liaison with an invisible UFOnaut after she had had a close sighting of an unidentified flying object. "I lay on my bed one night, just dozing off. Then I heard the steady tread of footsteps coming up the stairs. I knew the doors were locked and that I was alone. I lay there in fear, as the footsteps came closer and closer. At last they stopped beside my bed, and as the bedclothes were torn off my body, I wanted to scream, but could not. I lay unable to move as the thing lifted my nightgown and mounted me. I knew as only a woman can know that the thing was male."

Are some of our finest and brightest young women actually consorting with beings from other worlds, or have the incubi modernized their approach in order to seduce the more sophisticated of our technologically advanced maidens? Except for the sighting of the UFO prior to the visit of the bedroom invader, the letters which this author has received from serious and sincere young college and professional women might just as well have been accounts of our lusty, sexually aggressive incubus.

In *UFO Warning*,* New Zealand author John Stuart told of a sexual assault on his pretty young research assistant which came after the two of them had seen a grotesque, misshapen entity while investigating a UFO report. Stuart stated that he felt the young woman should have stayed with him and his wife, but she had insisted that she would be all right in her own home. Barbara, the young woman, had been incorrect.

She immediately noticed a peculiar odor the moment she stepped into her room. She undressed, bathed, but could not free her mind of the impression that unseen eyes followed her every move. Then, as she crushed out a cigarette and turned to put on her pajamas, an invisible something touched her on the shoulder. She found herself unable to move. The horror had begun.

For two and a half hours, an unseen entity had its way with her body.

"I concluded that the thing had been solid, even if invisible," Barbara told Stuart later. "There was, of course, no way of knowing exactly what it was like, and I tried to form a picture in my mind to fit it, but I gave up in fear. I got into bed and eventually fell into a deep sleep filled with nightmares. With the light of day, I again looked at my body and shuddered when I saw the scratches. It had really happened after all. . . ."

Barbara's flesh had been left covered with scratches from its contact with the rough-skinned space-age incubus.

* John Stuart, *UFO Warning*, Saucerian Books, Clarksburg, West Virginia.

Her ribs also bore two brown marks about the size of an American ten-cent piece. Barbara told Stuart that the thing had seemed only "clinically interested" in her body, as if it were engaging in sexual intercourse with an earth woman more out of curiosity than sensuality.

Quite understandably, Barbara lost her enthusiasm for UFO research after her terrifying other-worldly rape, and she moved to another city. A few weeks later, John Stuart himself came face to face with "it."

". . . Its body resembled, vaguely, that of a human. . . . Its flesh, stinkingly putrid, seemed to hang in folds. It was a grayish color. . . . The slack mouth was dribbling, and the horrible lips began to move, but there was no sound."

The creature communicated with Stuart telepathically and told him that thirteen of them had encircled Barbara on the night that she had been attacked, but only three of them had taken part in her sexual violation.

"Why did you scratch her?" Stuart asked angrily.

"It was something we couldn't avoid," the entity replied.

"Where did the two brown marks come from?" Stuart demanded.

"They are there to remind her of us," the thing responded.

Tarot reader Ron Warmoth told this author of a client of his who had also been given "marks" by which to remember her alleged extraterrestrial lover.

"I just looked at this woman in amazement when she told me that she was having sexual intercourse with a spaceman," Warmoth said. "She told me how she had seen a UFO and had established mental contact with one of the crewmen on board. Later, according to her, the spaceman had begun to materialize in her bedroom at night and make love to her."

The woman told the psychic that her other-worldly lover was well-versed in sexual techniques, but that his torrid embrace often left her with round burn marks. War-moth expressed some skepticism about the woman's story; then, before he could protest, the woman raised her skirt and displayed the evidence on her body.

"I can't say, of course, how the marks got there," War-moth told me, "but her inner thighs and her stomach were covered with small, round burns. It almost looked as if someone had placed a hot metal gridwork against her flesh."

John A. Keel, author of *Strange Creatures from Time and Space,* did two articles for popular magazines on certain aspects of the bedroom invaders and was amazed by the amount of mail which those pieces drew. "Many readers wrote to tell us, sometimes in absorbing detail, of their own experiences with this uncanny phenomenon," Keel said. "In most cases these experiences were not repetitive. They happened only once and were not accompanied by any other manifestations. In several cases the witnesses experienced total paralysis of the body. The witness awoke but was unable to move a muscle while the apparition was present. . . . Such visions could possibly be created by some kind of hypnotic process or by waves of electromagnetic energy which beam thought and impressions directly to the brain. This would mean that the experience was not entirely subjective but was caused by some inexplicable outside influence."

In a recent letter to this author, Keel stated: "It is my conclusion that cases of UFO sexual liaisons are actually a mere variation on the incubus phenomenon. Induced hallucinations seem to play a major role in these cases. There may be considerable validity to the theory you expounded in one of your books . . . that semen is extracted from human males in some succubi events and that this same semen is then introduced into human females in incubi incidents. The true nature and purpose of this operation is completely concealed behind a screen of deliberately deceptive induced hallucinations. Early fairy lore is filled with identical cases, as you know. And such sexual manipulations are an integral part of witchcraft lore."

Last year this author received a letter from a UFO percipient that related another example of the clinical interest certain flying-saucer occupants have in the sex act of *Homo sapiens*.

"Don't think I'm some kind of nut," the letter began in a familiar plea. "I never did believe in UFOs, but here is my experience. I will not reveal my name, but I live in Las Vegas. My hobby is women, and since I am married, I must be very careful.

"On July 2, 1968, a girl and I were parked on a very lonely desert road. We had a blanket on the ground and were very busy in a certain act, when a very, very hot wave fell on us. I looked up to see two men, both about five feet, six inches tall, standing beside us in a soft light. They had on some kind of coveralls that looked like diver suits. Their faces didn't look strange, but they had no hair on their heads. They spoke a language I couldn't understand. Behind them, hovering about twenty feet off the ground, was a craft that had a circle of small lights around its middle.

"The two men raised us up by our arms, and they felt all over our naked bodies. They pushed the backs of our knees and made us kneel, and one of them cut off some of my girl's hair and put it in a container and pointed toward the sky. Then they walked beneath the ship, stood in the circle of a spotlight, and they were gone. The UFO disappeared from sight in ten seconds."

Another percipient reported a similar lover's-lane experience in which two UFOnauts allegedly lifted him off his girl friend, milked his penis of semen, then hurried back to their hovering craft with their prize of human sperm sealed in a metallic container.

In the well-known case of Antonio Villas Boas in Brazil, a simple farm laborer claimed that he had been dragged off his tractor and into a UFO for the express purpose of impregnating a redhaired, fair-skinned, high-cheekboned, freckled female UFOnaut. The embarrassed farmer insisted that a love potion had weakened his resistance to the alien with the strangely slanted eyes, yet he stated with a touch of pride that he had been able to perform the sex act twice, in spite of the way she kept nibbling at him.

Mrs. Cynthia Appleton of Fentham Road, Aston, Birmingham, England, delivered a baby boy whose "spiritual father" was a Venusian. According to Mrs. Appleton, she had received a series of visits from the boy's "spiritual father," who simply appeared in her living room "like a blurred image on a TV screen, then everything is clear."

Ufologist Jerome Clark has told of encountering a twenty-one-year-old contactee in Minnesota who had been undergoing the plethora of eerie phenomena which researchers have come to expect—unexplained footsteps, knocking sounds, fainting spells that baffled the staff of a local hospital.

"But I like to return to one part of Martha Anderson's story when I feel myself getting too pessimistic about the nature of the intelligences behind the great enigma we are trying so desperately to solve," Clark said. "We picture the UFOnauts as somber, humorless creatures bent on the harmful manipulation of mankind, and we never suspect that they may be as weak as we are, victims of the same silly foibles and country-bumpkin mannerisms common to all of us who dwell on this celestial rock we call Earth."

One night Marty had awakened, shivering from a cold draft that had passed through her room. She sensed that she was not alone, and she lay on her stomach, her face pointed in the direction opposite to where she imagined the intruder stood. She had started to doze, when the sense of uneasiness returned. She felt someone lying next to her. She could not move, and she lay paralyzed with fright, waiting for something to happen.

"And then," Clark said, "quite without explanation, her brassiere unsnapped. And a moment later she knew that whoever or whatever had been there was gone. Perhaps alien beings capable of so preposterous, so pointless, so childish a gesture, need not be feared all that much."

10. LOVERS HAUNTED BY PHANTOMS AND NOISY GHOSTS

Although the poltergeist, that racketing bundle of projected repressions, is usually associated with the youth entering puberty and defining his sex role, such psychokinetic disturbances as the levitation of crockery and furniture and the materialization of voices and forms have been reported among newlyweds during their period of marital adjustment. The late psychoanalyst Dr. Nandor Fodor believed that the human body is capable of releasing energy in an unconscious and uncontrolled manner, thereby providing the power for the poltergeist's pranks. Author Sacheverell Sitwell agreed that the psychic energy for such disturbances usually comes from the psyche of someone undergoing sexual trauma. "The particular direction of this power is always toward the secret or concealed weaknesses of the spirit . . . the obscene or erotic recess of the soul," Sitwell conjectured.

A female medium told this author that she was capable of producing more phenomena when she was sexually frustrated. "Materializations, for example," she said. "I can produce stronger materializations and make them last longer if I am sexually frustrated or if I have become sexually aroused. I find it more difficult to conduct an ef-

fective séance if I am satisfied sexually; although sometimes during an especially good séance, I will reach orgasm
as I am producing a materialization.

"You [the author] generally see the poltergeist as a
psychological phenomenon. I can agree with this theory,
but I also believe that sexual frustration and longing, and
two young married kids trying to adjust to marriage, can
attract entities in many different forms. I do agree with
you privately—although I would probably deny it publicly
—that there is a strong link between sex and psychic phenomena."

If two young people who are experimenting with the
regenerative life force and learning to adjust to one another's sexual desires and needs are truly transmitting all
sorts of powerful vibrations, then it might seem within the
realm of possibility that certain of these life-force waves
might in some way reactivate old memory patterns which
have permeated "haunted" rooms. At the same time, these
sensual shock waves might stimulate the activity of certain
shadowy entities best left undisturbed.

Should the reader be willing to accept the thesis that two
young people in the throes of marital adjustment are capable of setting certain paranormal phenomena into psychokinetic motion, then he can imagine the phenomena
that might be produced by *three* newlywed couples living
under the same roof. Author M. G. Murphy provided the
editors of *Fate* with a notarized affidavit certifying to the
authenticity of the eerie events described by the six partici-
pants of such a haunted honeymoon.

The Murphys (author Murphy's parents), the Nelsons,
and the Chapmans found themselves with a common problem in February of 1917: the scarcity of money. They decided to find a house large enough so that each couple
would have their own bedroom, then cut down on expenses
by sharing the rent. After a period of house-hunting, they
found an immense three-story house on the outskirts of

Santa Ana, California, which rented for an absurdly small sum.

It took little time for the three couples to settle, for none of them had much furniture, and, strangely enough, the mansion had been rented fully furnished. Mrs. Murphy was an avid student of antiques, and she was overwhelmed by the splendid treasures the house contained. It seemed incredible that one could even consider renting out such a magnificent house complete with such valuable antiques, but the three young couples were not about to argue with Providence.

A few days after they had moved in, the three young wives were interrupted in their polishing of the paneled doors by the sound of someone running up the stairs. They had the full length of the stairway in their sight, yet they could hear the unmistakable sounds of someone clomping noisily up the stairs. Their report of the incident that night at dinner brought tolerant smiles from their husbands.

Several nights later the household was jolted out of sleep by Mrs. Nelson screaming that something was trying to smother her. While her husband sat ashen-faced with fear, she wrestled with an invisible assailant, until, finally, she was thrown to the floor with such force that her ankle twisted sickeningly beneath her and her head hit the wall. The doctor who was called to treat Mrs. Nelson's injuries mumbled something about it not being surprising considering the house they were living in; then he would say no more.

Within the next few days the footsteps continued to sound up and down the stairway. The men heard them too, and they also heard slamming doors and the splashing of water faucets being turned on. One night everyone saw the huge sliding doors pushed open by an invisible hand, and they all felt a cold breeze blow past them. When they locked the doors that night, one of the men observed that they were really locking up to protect the outside world from what they had on the inside. He was rewarded for his flippant observation by an incredibly foul, nauseating odor which hung about the stairway for days.

The three couples held a council to decide whether or not they should move. Although the disturbances were somewhat annoying, they reasoned, the rent simply could not be bettered. They would bear the bizarre phenomena and save their money.

The morning after their council had voted in favor of frugality, a new manifestation occurred which may have been designed to make them reconsider their decision. At the first glimmer of dawn, the couples awakened to the sound of a heavy wagon creaking up the driveway. They could hear the unmistakable sounds of shod hooves, jingling harness, and the murmur of men's voices. The phenomena, which culminated in an argument between two ghostly men, occurred at least twice a week thereafter.

When the three couples still gave no sign of moving, yet another disturbance was added to the repertoire of the haunting. Again, just before dawn, clanking sounds could be heard coming from an old rusted windmill at the rear of the house. There came the sound of a falling body that struck the metal structure on its way down, then came to rest with a heavy thud on the ground.

Mr. Murphy learned from some townspeople that a hired man had once fallen to his death from atop the windmill when a sudden gust of wind had swung the fan loose from its stabilizing brake. Apparently the three couples were being treated to an audio replay of the tragedy on alternating mornings with the creaking wagon and the argument.

One of the husbands discovered yet another phenomenon when he went into the basement to get a jar of fruit. Something knocked him off a box as he stood on tiptoe, reaching for the highest shelf, then lay sighing in a dark corner of the fruit cellar. The other two men stopped laughing at their friend when they followed him back down into the basement and heard the thing sighing and panting like a giant bellows.

Mrs. Murphy's grandparents came for a visit, and Grandmother Woodruff was quick to notice that there were "people" in the room with them. Grandmother Woodruff was a tiny woman who possessed great psychic abilities. In spite of her husband's violent disapproval of such activity, she had gained a great reputation as a "rainmaker" and a levitator of furniture and household objects. Grandmother Woodruff pointed to the portrait of the blond woman that hung above the fireplace and told the couples that the woman had been poisoned in one of the upstairs bedrooms. A frown from Grandfather Woodruff silenced her elaboration.

Later, when the others were gone, Mrs. Murphy asked her grandmother to attempt to gain additional psychic impressions. Grandmother Woodruff learned that something inhuman haunted the premises. "I'm not easily frightened," she said, "but whatever it is, I am terrified."

Just as the elderly couple were preparing to leave, some invisible monster threw Grandmother Woodruff to the floor before the fireplace and began to choke her. Grandmother's face was beginning to turn blue when Grandfather arrived to help her fight off the unseen foe. The thing slammed Grandmother to the floor when her husband called upon the name of God, and Grandfather Woodruff swept his gasping wife into his arms. Grandfather proclaimed the place a house of evil and advised them to move at once.

Grandmother Woodruff, whose voice was now but a rasping whisper, said that she had been "talking" to the blond lady when she had seen an awful creature creep up behind her. "It was as big as a man, but like nothing I've ever seen before. It had orange hair standing out from its head, stiff and wiry. Its hands curved into talons. The arms were like a man's, but covered with orange hair." The beast had threatened to kill Grandmother Woodruff, and it had left cuts on her neck where its talons had gouged into her flesh. "I know that this house will burn down within a short time. Nothing will be left but the foundation," she warned her granddaughter.

The three couples decided to move a few days later after a night during which a huge black bat had crept under the bedclothes and clamped its teeth into Mrs. Nelson's foot. It had taken two men to beat and to pry the monstrous bat off her foot, and even after it had been clubbed to the floor, it managed to rise, circle the room, and smash a window to escape.

Within a few weeks after the newlyweds left the mansion, it burned to the ground. The Murphy family's involvement with the hideous entity had not ended, however.

Ten years after Grandmother Woodruff's death, several of her kin were living in her old ranchhouse in San Bernardino. Author Murphy's Uncle Jim came downstairs ashenfaced one night and said that he had seen an orange-haired "thing" poke its head out of the storage room, then shut the door. Although the family laughed at him, Uncle Jim later complained of "something" in his room at nights. The gales of derisive laughter ceased when Uncle Jim died.

In 1948, Murphy's parents, who had been one of the three couples who had honeymooned in the accursed mansion, decided to spend their vacation on Grandmother Woodruff's old ranch. For company, they had the author's nine-year-old son Mike with them. Everything seemed comfortable in the old homestead on that first night, until, about 3:00 A.M., Mrs. Murphy was awakened by something shuffling toward Mike.

According to Murphy: "Looking it full in the face, Mother saw a grinning mouth with huge, yellow teeth. Its eyes were almost hidden in a series of mottled lumps. . . . Brushing her aside, it lunged toward Mike, who was now wide awake. Mother grabbed a handful of thick long hair and desperately clutched a hairy, scaly arm with the other.

In the moonlight which shone through the window she saw huge hands which curved into long talons. . . ."

By this time Mike was sitting up in bed screaming, watching helplessly as his grandmother did battle with the grotesque creature. At last Grandfather Murphy turned on the light in his room and came running to investigate the disturbance. The monster backed away from the light, but continued to gesture toward Mike.

In the light Mrs. Murphy could see that the beast wore ". . . a light-colored, tight-fitting one-piece suit of a thin material which ended at knees and elbow." Bristly orange hair protruded from its flattened and grossly misshapen nose, and thick, bulbous lips drew back over snarling yellow teeth. It gestured again in Mike's direction, then turned and shuffled through the doorway, leaving behind a sickening odor of decay.

Whether the entity had been attracted to the young couples by the tensions of their marital adjustment or whether it had been somehow activated by the vibrations of the life force emanating from their sexual activity cannot be answered. Although the phenomena began with somewhat ordinary poltergeistic disturbances, they seem to have culminated in either the creation of, or the attraction of, a violent and malignant entity. To the Murphys, at least, it has been demonstrated that creatures which haunt one house can, if they will it, move their operations along with the family. The old ranchhouse, the entity's last habitat, was razed in 1952.

Mrs. L. W. P. prepared a report of the manifestations which occurred in the small bungalow which she and her husband rented shortly after their marriage. They had only lived in the house about a week when she was disturbed by a strange thudding noise, "like someone striking an empty cardboard box with a closed fist."

She heard the noise several times over the next two weeks, and once it sounded not more than a few feet above her head. She began to have fainting spells, and when she regained consciousness, she would feel weak and drained of strength. She resisted telling her husband about the bizarre disturbances for fear of inviting his mockery. Her husband was a very materialistic young man who would not listen sympathetically to tales of things that went "bump" in an empty house.

Then one night when the newlyweds were hosting another young couple, Mrs. L. W. P. heard her husband calling her and the other woman from the kitchen, where they had been preparing a snack. "There's someone in the house," he said excitedly. Their guest substantiated his claim, and the two young couples set about searching the small home.

Mr. P. had said that as he and the other man had been sitting in the living room discussing an incident which had happened at work that day, a tall, blond, barefoot woman had pushed open the draperies and looked in at them. Her hair had seemed to be wet, and it stuck to her face. Both men had seen the woman clearly, and they had watched her bare feet under the draperies as she turned and walked away.

Since her husband had seen something for which he could not account, Mrs. L. W. P. unburdened herself and told them of the noises which had plagued her during the day and of the spells of fainting which had beset her in association with the thudding sounds.

"We lived in that house for just a few more weeks," Mrs. L. W. P. wrote in her account; "then we gave up and moved. We talked to a number of old-timers in the area who claimed that the place was haunted by the ghost of a woman who had been drowned by her husband. We were told that the place was always for rent or for sale. Many families had lived in the house, but none of them had stayed for more than a few weeks at a time."

Carol G. knew that, because of religious reasons, her

grandfather did not approve of Jack S. courting her. Grandpa G. had strong convictions that one should marry within one's faith, and it may have been the psychological tension which her grandfather created within her unconscious that led to a flurry of poltergeist activity around the teen-age girl.

For a period of nearly two weeks Jack's visits to the house were accompanied by violent outbursts of psychokinetic energy. Mrs. G.'s favorite vase shattered as the two young people held hands on the sofa. Invisible hands banged on the piano keyboard, and the piano stool jumped across the living-room floor and struck Carol smartly across the shins. One night as the young lovers had just finished making a tray of cookies and were allowing them to cool, the entire two dozen smoldered into flame. As in most poltergeist attacks, the unconscious energy center of the disturbance received the brunt of its abuse and physical torment. Stigmatalike scratches were seen to appear on Carol's upper arms, and on one occasion, teeth marks appeared just below her shoulderblades.

"You're to blame for this," Grandpa G. said one night, advancing upon Jack with his cane. "To mix religions is to do the devil's work, and you've brought the devil upon us."

The old man swung his cane and caught Jack stoutly across the forehead. Jack jumped to his feet, dazed, angry, but restrained by his sweetheart. "If you were thirty years younger," Jack said, grimly clenching his fists.

The poltergeist activity eventually spent its psychic energy, and the vortex of paranormal disturbances subsided. In spite of Grandpa G.'s fulminations, Carol's parents were open-minded toward a religiously mixed marriage and gave their consent for the young people to be wed. Grandpa G. contracted pneumonia a month before the wedding date and passed away in an oxygen tent in the hospital. In spite of their differences over religion and her choice of a husband, Carol was genuinely sorrowful when the old man died.

A few psychic strands of unconscious guilt over marrying outside her religion and against her grandfather's wishes may have produced the phenomena that visited Carol on her wedding night.

The newlyweds had checked into the nearest possible motel, eager to consummate their marriage. They had no sooner gone to bed, however, when they were sharply distracted from the marital rite by a loud knocking on the wall beside them. They tried desperately to ignore the sound, to blame it on a raucous party next door, but the more they listened to the rapping, the more they both realized that it sounded very much like Grandpa G.'s cane.

As they watched in amazement, a glowing orb of light appeared beside their bed. As the illumination grew and took shape, they were astonished to see a wispy outline of Carol's grandfather standing before them.

"He . . . he's smiling," Carol said, somehow managing to shape functional speech in her fear and surprise.

As the newlyweds lay in each other's arms, they saw the image of Grandpa G. smile, move his cane in the sign of the cross, then in a gesture of farewell. "He's blessed us, Jack," Carol said, tears welling in her eyes as she watched the ethereal form of her grandfather fade away. "He understands now that he's on the other side. Earthly differences don't matter over there."

Mrs. L. J. J. has prepared an account of an experience which occurred to her and her fiancé shortly before their marriage. They had gone to a movie, then decided to drive out to the tiny house in the country where they would live after they had celebrated their nuptials.

"It was fun to go there and plan our future," she said. "The house was on land that was too wooded to be good farmland, but we planned only to plant a small garden, and Karl would continue his job in town.

"We had only kerosene lamps in those days, but they always gave off such a cheery light—at least, they usually did. That night, when Karl lit the lamp, I had an eerie feeling that something was wrong, that we were not alone. Karl must have felt the same way as I did, because he kept looking over his shoulder, like he expected to catch sight of someone spying on us.

" 'I'm going to have a look around,' he said, trying to sound casual. He took the lamp, so I stayed right beside him. We walked through the small house, and Karl grinned at me sheepishly, as if he were apologizing for feeling uneasy in what was to be our honeymoon cottage.

"We heard a strange chattering, like some giant squirrel or chipmunk, coming from a dark corner in the room. It sounded unreal, unearthly, and a strange coldness passed over my body. 'Let's go, Karl,' I whispered. 'I'm frightened.'

"Before we could move toward the door, Karl suddenly threw his hands up over his head as if he were trying to grab something behind him. His head seemed pulled backward and to one side. His mouth froze in a grimace of pain and fear, and his eyes rolled wildly. He lost balance, fell to his knees, then to his side. He kicked over a chair as he rolled madly, fighting and clawing the air around his neck.

"I stood by helplessly, stunned with fear and bewilderment. Karl managed to struggle to his feet. His eyes bulged and he gasped fiercely for each breath. Some unseen thing seemed to be strangling him.

" 'The door . . . open . . . run to car . . . you drive,' he panted. We ran to the car, Karl stumbling, staggering as if something heavy and strong were perched atop his shoulders with a death grip about his throat. 'I . . . can't get . . . damned thing off!'

"I got behind the wheel of the car. 'Drive . . . fast!' Karl said, his hands desperately trying to pry the invisible monster's paws from his throat.

"I drove for about two miles down the road. Suddenly there was a blinding flash inside the car. A brilliant ball of fire about the size of a basketball shot ahead of our car, then veered sharply to the left and disappeared into a clump of trees.

"I did not stop all the way back to town. Karl lay gasping beside me, his head rolling limply on the back of the seat. He did not speak until we were back inside the city limits. 'It was some inhuman thing from the pits of hell,' he said. 'It was big, strong, and it would have killed me.' "

Mrs. L. J. J. concluded her account by writing that although they returned to their small home with some trepidation, they never again encountered that monstrous, invisible strangler that chattered like a giant rodent.

Not all phantoms encountered by young lovers are of the violent, noisy variety. Some phantoms seem to materialize simply to observe, maybe even to protect.

A young woman recently presented this author with an account of an incident which occurred to her when she was seventeen years old and uninitiated into the mysteries of sex. "It was during the holiday season," she stated, "just after Christmas. I was visiting my brother in a strange town and meeting all of his friends. Due to space limitations and other factors, I could not stay with my brother, but I did find a room in a boardinghouse where many of his friends lived."

Jennie had just become settled when she was told that the room had been promised to another for the following week and she would have to move. An older man invited her to stay with him in his apartment, and Jennie was faced with a rather delicate dilemma. She had promised her parents that she would be a "good girl" on the trip, and she wondered if it were possible to remain virginal while sharing an apartment with an older, experienced man. She checked Rob out with her brother, and he told her that Rob was a gentleman and had two bedrooms in his apartment. Big brother seemed confident that Rob would not take advantage of little sister.

"Rob was a gentleman," Jennie agreed in her report,

"but there was also a great deal of warmth and affection between us, and I never did sleep in his spare bedroom. We slept together in his big bed, and he chose not to take advantage of the little virgin sleeping beside him.

"But one night his masculine drive refused to be quieted. He told me the next morning how he had lain awake on his back, fighting his desire. He was excruciatingly aware of my presence beside him. I was sound asleep and oblivious to the sexual torment he was going through.

"At last he could stand it no longer, Rob told me later. He rolled to his side and looked at me intently. He reached out to touch me, to move me over on my back—then he looked up in astonishment. There, seated beside me and gazing protectively down at me, was the Virgin Mary. Blue cloth partly shielded her face, and she never removed her eyes from my face.

"Rob rolled again to his back and felt the desire ebb from his body. Rob had been raised a Roman Catholic, and though he had abandoned its more ritualistic precepts for the psychic-spiritist approach to spiritual matters, the figure of the Virgin had deeply moved him.

"The next morning the two of us discussed the vision, and we both decided that it had not been the actual Virgin Mary smiling down on me, but the personification of the ideal of virginity protecting me. The psychic manifestation had chosen that particular form as a symbol which would have great emotional impact on Rob.

"We also decided that, for the duration of my stay, at least, my maidenhead would remain intact."

11. INVISIBLE DEMONS
THAT POSSESS AND DESTROY

The skeptics say with finality that the evil thoughts and the emotions of the living or the dead cannot overpower the healthy brain of a normal person. The mind cannot be subdued unless by physical distortion or disease.

There are intelligent men and women who feel otherwise. They are convinced that they have felt the touch of demons. In their experience, the admonition, "Get thee behind me, Satan," is by no means a fanciful directive. Serious individuals claim to have undergone fearsome ordeals in which either they or their loved ones became the targets of vile entities which sought the possession of physical bodies and minds in order that they might enjoy the sensations of demonically aroused mortals who yield to ungodly temptations.

The skeptical will dismiss such stories as examples of psychological disorders, but certain psychical researchers and those who have been victimized argue that demonic possession is not insanity, for in most cases the possession is only temporary. The individual who has become possessed is unable to control himself, although he may be entirely conscious of the fiendish manipulation of his mind and body, and in many instances he may actually see grotesque and devilish faces before him.

Author Ed Bodin tells of the possession of beautiful Yvonne Marchand, the daughter of Colonel Marchand, the French officer who had been sent to take command of the French detachment in Indochina in 1923. The lovely blond eighteen-year-old had become the belle of the military colony, and Colonel Marchand's troubles seemed few. Although he was of the old military school and contemptuous of native beliefs, the natives, for the most part, tolerated him.

The colonel's principal error in public relations lay in the area of what he adjudged native trespassing on military property. A native corporal explained to the officer that the reason for such regular trespassing could be found in the people's desire to avoid going through a certain demon-possessed swamp to get to the hills beyond. According to native legend, he who passed through the swamp at night would become possessed of fiendish demons. Colonel Marchand found only amusement in such an account.

One day a native thief surrendered, rather than seek escape by running into the accursed swamp. Colonel Marchand decided to demonstrate the qualities of French mercy, so rather than having the man shot, he ordered him cast into the midst of the swamp, so that the thief would have to wade through the area he so feared. The felon begged the colonel to reconsider, and he attempted to throw himself at the feet of the colonel's daughter to beseech her understanding. All he accomplished, unfortunately, was to trip Yvonne. In a rage, the officer had the man forced into the swamp at bayonet point.

That night Yvonne's maid rushed to the colonel with the news of the thief's terrible revenge. He had managed to creep back into camp, and he had carried off the colonel's daughter. A search was immediately organized, but the native corporal feared the worst when the trail led to the swamp.

A soldier met the search party at the edge of the swamp. The thief had been found bleeding to death, his face and body covered with scratches, his jugular vein torn open. With his dying words he had gasped that the beautiful Yvonne had wrenched herself free of his grasp and had turned on him with her teeth and nails.

The men searched an hour with powerful spotlights and lanterns before they caught sight of something white moving ahead of them in the swamp. It was Yvonne, naked except for a strip of cloth about her thighs. The searchlight caught the streaks of blood on her body, but her father was most horrified by her face. A fiendish grin parted her lips, and her teeth flashed as if she were some wild thing waiting for prey to fall within reach of claw and fang. She rushed the nearest soldier, ready to gouge and bite.

Colonel Marchand ran to his daughter's side. She eluded his grasp, seemed about to turn on him, then collapsed at his feet. Her shoulders and breasts were covered with the indentations of dozens of tooth marks. The colonel covered his daughter's nakedness from the curious gaze of the soldiers, and he called for a litter with which to have Yvonne carried home.

Later, when the girl regained consciousness, she told a most frightening and bizarre story. The thief had clamped a hand over her mouth and dragged her into the swamp. When he had stopped to rest, Yvonne had become aware of horrible faces bobbing all around them.

"A terrible sensation came over me," the girl said. "Never before have I felt anything like it. I wanted only to kill the man, to bite his throat, to tear at his face. I have never had such strength before. I mangled him as if he were a child. I gloried in ripping his flesh, in seeing him drop to the ground and crawl away. Then the faces summoned me on into the swamp. I tore off my clothes and began to bite myself. The faces laughed at me, and I laughed too."

When Yvonne had seen the lights of the searchers, she became angry and had wanted to kill them. "And, Father," she went on, "I knew you, but I wanted to kill you too. I kept trying to think of you as my father, but something kept tearing at my brain. Then, when you reached out to touch me, the awful fire that was burning inside me seemed to fall away."

Thereafter, Colonel Marchand was much more sympathetic to the hill people who trespassed across a small portion of military property to avoid the swamp. His daughter had said over and over again that if there truly were a hell, that swamp must be it. Eventually the swamp was completely filled in by earth and stone from a more godly spot of ground. Yvonne Marchand bore no lasting ill effects of her ordeal and later married and produced healthy children. But when friends got her to tell of her night of possession in the Indochinese swamp, few walked away as skeptics.

Caroline Spencer is a nurse who specializes in private care. Two years ago she received a job offer from a young businessman whose wife had become crippled in a hunting accident. The couple had no children, and the wife was lonely, as well as in need of professional care. "My wife is an absolute saint," the man told Miss Spencer over the telephone. "She never complains."

When Miss Spencer arrived at their residence, the husband had already left on a three-day business trip. She let herself in with the key that had been sent to her, and she found the woman, Mrs. Eston, in her bedroom. "Hello, Caroline, baby," the woman greeted her, a strange smile stretching her lips in a leer. "Oh, my, we are going to get along just fine."

Miss Spencer was surprised at the display of familiarity upon their first meeting. She asked Mrs. Eston how she had learned her first name, and the woman told her that she knew lots of things about her. "Her eyes had a strange cast to them," Miss Spencer said in her report. "There almost seemed to be a flame flickering behind each of them."

Miss Spencer put in an exhausting first night. Every few minutes Mrs. Eston would summon her to her bedside on some pretext, then complain loudly about the nurse's general incompetence. When Miss Spencer suggested that they should both get some sleep, Mrs. Eston laughed and said, "I don't need to sleep, and you, my dear, are not going to get any!"

The next morning, Mrs. Eston mocked her by telling her how tired and worn-out she looked. "You could use a beauty nap, my dear."

Miss Spencer could not wait to meet Mr. Eston in person and let him have a piece of her mind. So his wife was a saint, eh? So his wife never complained, eh? She decided to call Mrs. Eston's doctor and arrange for some tranquilizers for the woman so she could get some rest. When the nurse explained her problem to the doctor, he expressed his amazement and said that he would stop by on his way home to lunch.

The nurse had no sooner cradled the receiver when she heard a deep male voice singing an obscene song. Miss Spencer put a weary hand to her throbbing forehead. The voice was coming from Mrs. Eston's room. Had the "saint" taken herself a coarse lover to while away the long hours in bed? Although the accident had crippled her, she remained a breathtakingly attractive woman, albeit a bit emaciated.

"For a moment I thought I was losing my mind," Miss Spencer said. "The deep, foul voice was coming from Mrs. Eston's own throat. 'So you called the doctor, huh?' the voice said grimly. 'You're a tattletale, honey, but you are going to be in for a surprise.'

"When the doctor arrived, Mrs. Eston was completely composed, and she spoke in cultured, well-modulated tones. She was sweet, pleasant, the very picture of the long-suffering, ideal patient. The doctor stopped for a cup of coffee with me before he left. He tried to make the conversation about medical schools and courses of study sound casual and shop-talkish, but I knew that he was sounding me out about my background. Behind his pleasant, professional smile, he was questioning my qualifications as a private nurse. Before he left, he told me that he could see no reason to prescribe tranquilizers for Mrs. Eston, and in his brusque manner, suggested that I could benefit more than she from such a prescription."

As soon as the doctor had left, the deep voice began howling with laughter and delivered foul curses at Miss Spencer. The nurse walked back to the bedroom, looked deep into the black, glittering eyes. "Why do you do such things, Mrs. Eston?" was all she could manage, and the strange woman mocked her for her weakness.

For two nights Miss Spencer bore the curses and imprecations of the deep voice that boomed from within the frail, crippled woman. Once when the nurse was attempting to bathe her, Mrs. Eston's hand shot out to grasp her by the throat. Miss Spencer nearly blacked out before she managed to wrest the powerful fingers from her throat.

"You're a strong woman," the deep voice said approvingly, as the nurse sat gasping on the floor. "How are you in bed, honey? Can you show a man a good time? If I could get these legs working, I would sure in hell find out."

Miss Spencer looked up in horror at the black eyes that looked down on her with such evil appraisal. Dimly, in the back of her mind, strange thoughts were beginning to collect, thoughts long ago banished by her scientific training.

"You beginning to get the picture now, honey?" the voice asked. "Mrs. Eston, hell! You come close to me again, and you'll find out who I really am!"

That night the foul voice stopped shouting selections from what seemed to be an inexhaustible supply of filth. Miss Spencer could hear the sound of soft crying coming from Mrs. Eston's room. When she investigated, she found the woman lying in a state of confusion.

"Who are you?" Mrs. Eston demanded in a weak voice. "Where's my husband? What's happening to me? Oh, nurse, whoever you are, please keep that ugly brute away from me!"

Miss Spencer fed Mrs. Eston some soup, took advantage of the lull to bathe her. She talked soothingly to the woman, and when she had left Mrs. Eston so that they might both get some rest, she allowed the terrible thought to escape from the corner of her brain where she had kept it chained: *Mrs. Eston was possessed.*

If Miss Spencer had hoped for sleep that night, there was none to be had. She had just lain down to rest when she heard Mrs. Eston vomiting. "No food for you, bitch!" roared the deep voice over and over again in between the sounds of the woman retching. "And no rest for you until I stop your heart!"

Miss Spencer ran to the woman with cold cloths, but she was given no opportunity to clean the mess. "Let her lie in filth and vomit," the angry voice warned her. "Let the bitch die. You come closer, and I'll wring your silly neck!"

"No," Miss Spencer said, "I know what you are now. With God's help, I'll do my duty." The nurse spoke on of God's love and of how God answered prayers. The thing that had invaded Mrs. Eston clamped palms to her ears and screamed that it would not listen to such talk. While it was thus distracted, Miss Spencer cleaned up the vomit that had spewed out of the woman.

When Mr. Eston returned that next day, Miss Spencer's haggard appearance told him that his worst fears had been realized. He begged the nurse's forgiveness. "I thought . . . I hoped she might be different for you," he said by way of explanation.

At Miss Spencer's prompting, Mr. Eston told of how they had found his wife's body lying inside an old stone hut on that day of the hunting accident. No one could ever understand why she had gone into the hut or how she had accidentally shot herself. The only theory they had developed was that she had set her shotgun against a wall and it had slipped off the moist rock and gone off when it had struck the floor. The pellets had damaged her spine and had rendered her paralyzed from the waist down. The nature of the hut? Nothing special, just an old house where some nutty old recluse had lived and died hating mankind.

"And now," Mr. Eston said, fighting to hold back tears, "my poor wife has been transformed into some incredible kind of lunatic. How that deep voice comes out of her, I'll never understand."

At almost the same instant, Miss Spencer and Mr. Eston realized that it had become silent in his wife's room. "Let me check," the nurse told the anxious husband.

"I shall never forget that sight," Miss Spencer wrote. "I have seen death in many manifestations, but I know I shall never see the equal of what I saw in that room. Mrs. Eston's facial features were distorted into an expression of malignant evil. The face lying on that pillow resembled that of a gargoyle or some hideous demon. Somehow I managed to check for pulse and respiration. There was none. I returned to Mr. Eston and told him that he should not enter the bedroom. He would never have recognized the features of his once-beautiful wife.

"Later I learned that Mrs. Eston had been buried quietly with a closed-casket funeral. The mortician had worked for several hours on her face, but her features continued to slip back into that horrible grimace. Whatever had possessed Mrs. Eston had won a physical victory. I only pray that it had not been able to claim the woman's soul as well as her body."

12. STRANGE PHENOMENA
THAT DISTURB PREGNANT
WOMEN

Rosemary was not the only expectant mother who had terrible premonitions about her baby. According to dream researchers, thousands of mothers-to-be have dreams of giving birth to grotesque demons and hideous monsters.

Dr. Stanley Krippner, who served as the director of the William C. Menninger Dream Laboratory at Maimonides Medical Center in Brooklyn, New York, said: "We have found a large percentage of pregnant women who dream about giving birth to deformed babies and monsters, and they had these dreams long before *Rosemary's Baby* became a best-selling novel and a popular motion picture. These dreams express a natural fear that something will go wrong with the unborn child. So many mothers have these dreams that we do not consider them to be pathological in most cases."

In research conducted by Diane R. Schneider, with the co-sponsorship of Dr. William Pomcranre, director of the Maimonides Hospital obstetrics department, it was determined that pregnancy, the wish for pregnancy, and the fear of pregnancy actually influence dream content to a high degree.

Dr. R. L. Van de Castle, research consultant to Miss

Schneider's project, noted that, occasionally, a woman may have a dream which accurately foresees the future in regard to her pregnancy and her delivery. Dr. Van de Castle discovered one woman who claimed that she had had recurring nightmares for several years, ever since the time she had seen illustrations of an abnormal fetus in her fiancé's medical textbook.

The woman said that her dreams were always identical. She lay in a hospital bed in hard labor. Her sister was always in the dream, and she, too, was in the terminal stages of gestation. The dream always ended the same way. Her sister would give birth to a healthy, normal child, and the dreamer, after long, excruciating labor, would bear a deformed baby.

The woman suffered through the dreams for nearly six years before she married and became pregnant for the first time. "Then I knew instinctively and absolutely that the pregnancy would repeat itself identically with the dream," she told Dr. Van de Castle. "And it did, even to my sister actually being pregnant at the same time that I was."

As in the recurring dream, the woman's sister gave birth to a healthy, normal girl, while she bore a deformed stillborn child.

When the woman became pregnant again a year later, her doctor warned her to expect a psychologically difficult pregnancy because of her previous experience. "But I assured him that now the dream had lived itself out in reality, there would be no more worry on my part," the woman said. "The dream never recurred, and I gave birth to a normal child."

Mrs. M. J.'s precognitive dream had a happier message, and because the young woman believed in its declaration, she saved the life of her unborn child.

Mrs. M. J. was in her second month of pregnancy when her doctor advised her that she must have an abortion. In his opinion, it would be fatal for her to bear the child. At her husband's urging, the woman made the necessary arrangements to be aborted legally. Then, the night before the operation, she had a dream in which an angel appeared before her holding a handsome baby boy in his arms. On the strength of that dream, Mrs. M. J. refused the abortion and carried the baby full term. Seven months later, she gave birth to the smiling baby boy she had seen so vividly in her dream.

When Mrs. E. R. was pregnant, she and her husband lived with in-laws, and she charitably described their arrangement as "an unhappy situation." Whenever she had had a particularly trying day, Mrs. E. R. would experience the same beautiful dream in which she was walking among lovely flowers with a little girl at her side and soothing, uplifting music playing in the background.

After her little girl was born and they had moved into a home of their own, the beautiful dream ceased, but Mrs. E. R. often thought of it. When her daughter was about five, Mrs. E. R. took the girl along to a flower show that was being held at a convention hall in a nearby city. The entire hall had been transformed into a lovely, fragrant garden, and an orchestra played soothing, uplifting music.

"Suddenly it struck me," Mrs. E. R. wrote in her report of the paranormal experience. "This was my dream, that beautiful, tension-relieving dream that I had had when I was pregnant!"

The most remarkable facet of this particular report occurred when her daughter tugged at Mrs. E. R.'s skirt, her eyes sparkling excitedly, and said: *"We've* been here lots and lots of times before, haven't we, Mommy?" Psychologists have only begun to explore the many subtle, unconscious links which exist between the expectant mother and the child she nurtures in her womb.

The physical process of pregnancy seemed to develop latent mediumistic abilities in Mrs. K. F. At first she thought she must be going insane when she began to see men and women walking through her house when she knew absolutely without a doubt that she was home alone. Fortunately, she had done some reading in the field of psychic phenomena and the paranormal, and she had managed to properly evaluate the strange occurrences before she began to communicate with certain of the entities. Then, too, the ability to perceive glimpses through a window into another world seemed to occur only when she had had a day filled with anxiety or tension.

When her baby was born, Mrs. K. F. sensed that the child was not as healthy as the doctor's forced cheerfulness was supposed to lead her to believe. The nurses were just too attentive to suit her, too. One night, just before feeding time, Mrs. K. F. lay flipping idly through the pages of her magazine, waiting impatiently to have her full breasts milked by her son. She hoped that the poor little thing would be able to keep down more milk tonight.

She heard footsteps approaching her bed, and thinking it was the nurse, Mrs. K. F. reached over to set her magazine on the bedstand. She was surprised to see her grandmother, who had been dead for seven years, holding her son in her plump arms. "I'm sorry, honey," her grandmother told her, "but I've had to come for your baby. Don't fret, 'cause I'll take real good care of him."

A half-hour later, the head nurse pushed open the door to Mrs. K. F.'s room. "You don't have to tell me," Mrs. K. F. said, managing to control her voice. "I know that my baby's dead."

"The doctor tried," the nurse said, not stopping to puzzle over Mrs. K. F.'s knowledge of her child's death. "He worked over him until . . ."

"Until Great-Grandmother came to take him," Mrs. K. F. finished.

One of my young correspondents spent some time with an Eastern seacoast colony of painters, artists, poets, writ-

ers, and visionaries. While there, she came across this interesting account of a pregnant haunted lover.

Liz, a painter, and Gabe, a singer, had begun living together in Florida, and by the time they moved farther
north, Liz was pregnant with Gabe's child. Both young people were tuned into the paranormal, but they approached
the field with different ideals.

Liz began to practice cosmic motherhood toward her
unborn babe, and she believed that her thoughts and medi-
tations would influence the character and the personality
of the developing soul within her womb. She frequented
health-food stores, meditated daily, and tried to live a spiritual life.

Gabe, on the other hand, became increasingly involved
in the lower aspects of psychism. He could not hide his fas-
cination for a certain young woman, variously labeled by
those who knew her as "an acid freak," "a black witch,"
or "a very sick girl." The loosely organized coven that met
under the young witch's directorship began, somewhat ig-
norantly, yet consciously, toying with the Left Hand side of
psychism.

At this point, while Liz sought spiritual development and
Gabe sought psychic kicks, the young couple were still un-
married. Gabe fled from the approaching responsibility of
fatherhood, and Liz was forced to spend nearly every night
alone in the strange town. Finally, when Liz was in her
seventh month of pregnancy, Gabe proposed marriage.

The vocalization of his commitment to the pregnant girl
did little to domesticate the reluctant father, however. In
spite of numerous tearful sessions, Liz could not convince
Gabe to stay at home and give her the crucial support and
love that she so desperately needed. She began losing
sleep, worried by her awareness that a woman in her
seventh month of pregnancy presented scant competition
for the pretty hippie chicks who frequented the coffee
houses where Gabe sang.

One night Liz was having a particularly hard time. In an

effort to suppress her feelings, she began to sketch. She drew a line, then another, and suddenly began to draw in earnest. Liz had never liked to draw people, but there, slowly filling up the sheet of paper, was the face of an attractive young girl. Liz began to receive impressions about the girl. She knew that the image was an exact rendering, and she knew that the girl was very young, no more than fifteen.

As Liz stared at the portrait she had wrought, the paper became a swirling, fuzzy mass of images. Liz shook her head to clear it of its sudden lightness. Lights and colors passed before her eyes. Then images were forming on the paper, as if the sketchpad had been suddenly transformed into a television set.

There was Gabe. He was driving in their car with someone Liz could not see clearly. Gabe drove up to a motel and got out of the car. Liz strained to see who his companion was. The car door opened, and the young girl whose portrait Liz had just drawn stepped out. Although she loathed witnessing her fiancé's infidelity, Liz could not tear her clairvoyant eyes from the paper. Like an unseen voyeur, she watched Gabe take the young girl to bed and make love to her.

Gabe returned to their apartment at daybreak, and Liz lost no time in confronting him with his unfaithfulness. When Gabe denied any knowledge of what she was talking about, Liz waited her moment, then flashed the portrait in his face. He blanched visibly, strove to regain his composure, but his eyes could not keep from straying toward the portrait of his current paramour.

An hour later, the doorbell rang. Since Gabe was angrily hunched over on his side of the bed still vehemently denying everything, Liz got up to answer the door.

The sight of their caller almost made Liz recoil against the doorframe. There, wearing a simpering expression, was the young girl whom she had first drawn, then "seen" with

Gabe at the motel. "Is Gabe home?" the girl wanted to know.

Liz made an expansive sweep of her arm, noted with grim satisfaction that the girl had become suddenly subdued. The girl was intelligent enough to assess the role that Liz, very obviously with child and very obviously with swollen red eyes, played in Gabe's life. The teeny-bopper turned from the door and walked away.

"And the most amazing part of the whole story," my young correspondent wrote, "is that Liz still married Gabe!"

In March of 1969, this author received a handwritten letter in which all words were connected in a heavy, penciled scrawl. "Dear Brad Steiger, For some reason I seem compelled to write to you. I don't know why, but I guess I must at this time. We . . ." And then, with the exception of a word here and there, the rest of the connected and chaotic words were illegible. The last few lines and the signature were nothing but blurred scribbles. Although I receive a great deal of mail from readers of my books and magazine articles, I do not really harvest very many "kook" letters, and somehow I felt that this woman was sincere in her helpless scrawlings, that she wanted help.

A few days later I found that my impression had proved to be correct, for I received a letter from a gentleman who identified himself as my previous correspondent's husband. According to him, his wife had been given a drug for postnatal blues that, in her case, had acted as a hallucinogenic and had expanded her consciousness so widely that they were involved in a maelstrom of psychic activity that included, in his words, "just about everything Brad Steiger has ever written about in his books." Since her husband had begun reading in the field, he was foresighted enough to realize the value of keeping a record of all that transpired in their apartment during the psychic siege. I was fortunate enough to receive this journal with the husband's additional notes for use in my research. I shall quote a few examples from the notebook to indicate the wide range of paranormal phenomena which centered around the new mother in her drug-induced state of awareness.

HALLUCINATIONS—A. C. was aware of huge eyes and faces floating about the room. These eyes, she termed "The Watchers," and she was convinced that they were spying on them at all times.

CLAIRVOYANCE—She could literally see through walls and look in on others in their apartments. Once A. C. saw that a woman several apartments away had gone on a brief errand and left her children unattended. A. C. went down to the apartment, found that this was so, and sat with the children until their mother returned.

PRECOGNITION—When the telephone would ring, A. C. would tell her husband who would be on the line, and what the party wished. "Once she told me that D. B. would call and ask me to build a store on our lot and lease it to him," her husband said. "Within a short time, D. B. did call and make exactly that proposition to me."

A. C. regularly read the front pages of the newspaper days in *advance*. She "saw" a large block of ice fall off an awning and kill a man in a nearby city three days before the actual occurrence was reported in the press. She also saw a fire break out in a local hospital and begged her husband to warn the personnel of the spreading flames. She did not relax until the scream of fire engines told her that the fire had been detected.

PSYCHOKINESIS—"Listen," A. C. would say, as she pointed to the vacant apartment above them, "hear the spies walking around?" Although the apartment was empty, her husband testified, "The moment she would declare footsteps walking up there, we would hear those footsteps. If she would say 'loud' footsteps, they would be loud. If she said they were 'tiptoeing,' they would be barely audible. Then she might say, 'They've taken our telephone off the hook so they can listen to us!' And sure enough, whenever she said that, I would walk out to the other room and find the receiver off the cradle."

UNUSUAL STRENGTH—Mr. C. is a husky, former all-state football player. It was a trifle humiliating for him to find that he could not restrain his wife on one occasion when she wished to get out of bed. "She had all these stitches and was supposed to lie quietly," he said. "She pushed me away as if I were a child, because she wanted to do *sit-ups* to flatten her tummy and get her figure back. Once she punched me so hard in the jaw that I was literally knocked clear across the room and flipped backwards over a chair."

OUT-OF-BODY-EXPERIENCE—A. C. recalls leaving her body on several occasions and traveling unrestrained through space. "That was how I knew so many things before they were reported in the newspapers," she said. "I would fly over to Europe and England and Russia and see the events occurring before they hit the American press."

Although the worst of the paranormal plague passed in about two months, it took a year for the drug to leave A. C.'s system. Each month during the time of her period, the apartment would once again be visited by psychokinetic disturbances, such as the sound of footsteps, the rattling of pictures, and on one occasion, Mr. C. believes, there may have been a manifestation of a globe of glowing light, because he could find no natural or reflected source for the illumination. Just a few weeks before the writing of this chapter (April, 1970), I received a call from Mr. C. "Well, Brad," he said, "I think we've made it. A.'s period is here, and this time we have no footsteps and no rattling pictures!"

13. OUT-OF-BODY LOVE AND LUST

Mrs. Carlyle Basso's husband is a construction worker, who one time, due to unemployment in the area, was forced to take a job on a large dam project more than four hundred miles from his home.

"It was the longest six months I think I have ever spent," Mrs. Basso wrote. "Carlyle could only get home on weekends. He would not arrive home until after midnight on Friday, and he would have to be back on the road right after the noon meal on Sunday. For those six months, we only lived on Saturdays."

Mrs. Basso remembered one dreary fall day when she was particularly lonely. The clouds hung low in the sky and drizzled on the multicolored leaves at sporadic intervals. It was the kind of day to share with someone you love. She felt lonely and depressed, but she pulled on a heavy sweater and sat in her cold house pasting premium stamps in their appropriate books.

"That night my bed felt as cold, damp, and lonely as a grave," Mrs. Basso said. "My only consolation was that it was Thursday and Carlyle would be home that next night. I lay shivering between the sheets, cursing the job situation that had taken my husband so far away from me.

"Then I thought that I felt a slight pressure on Carlyle's side of the bed. I turned over, saw nothing, but it seemed to me that I could feel a kind of warmth coming from my husband's pillow. I ran my hand along the inside of the bedclothes, and I concluded that I must be losing my grip on reality—Carlyle's side of the bed definitely felt warm, like he had been sleeping there and had just got up.

"I lay on my side of the bed for a few moments longer, then, once again, I slid my hand over the sheet. There could be no mistaking it. The bed on Carlyle's side was as warm as toast. It had been a cold, lonely day, and I had no interest in trying to figure out why that side of the bed should be so warm when no one was sleeping there. Without another moment's hesitation, I slid over into the blessed pocket of warmth and comfort and fell asleep almost at once.

Mrs. Basso did not think of the strange incident again until she and her husband were eating their farewell Sunday meal. Carlyle's response to her curious story was hardly what she had expected. He stared at her for a few moments in complete silence, then spoke to her in slow, measured sentences.

Carlyle Basso had been lying in the construction workers' bunkhouse on that Thursday night, trying to come to terms with his loneliness. If he had had his own car, he told his wife, he would have chucked it all, job or no job, and come home to her right then. That night as he lay there surrounded by his snoring companions, his entire being seemed suffused with personal anguish. He wanted so much to be in his own clean bed, to be able to feel his wife sleeping beside him.

"I decided to experiment," he told his wife. "I wanted to see if it were possible to will myself home over those four hundred miles. I rested my hands behind my head and summoned every drop of concentration that I had inside my brain. I thought of nothing but you and home.

"There was a kind of rushing sensation, and I stood beside our bed looking down at you. You were just lying there, looking kind of sad, not yet sleeping. I slipped in beside you, and you moved your hand over me. A few minutes later, you did it again. I thought that you knew I lay there, because you rolled over and snuggled up next to me. I put my arm around you, and we both went right to sleep."

Carlyle awakened back in the bunkhouse that next morning, just as his wife awakened alone in her bed back home. "But we will always wonder if Carlyle really did come home that night," Mrs. Basso wrote, "or if our deep love enabled us to share a dream so that we could experience a moment of comfort when we were both longing so terribly for one another."

A growing number of scientific researchers are becoming convinced that such experiences as that described above by Mr. and Mrs. Carlyle Basso may truly be more than dreams. The phenomenon of leaving one's body to float off in spirit to the ceiling, to another room, or, in some cases, to another city or country, is known as out-of-body experience.

Dr. Charles Tart, a psychologist and lecturer at the University of California in Sacramento, has noted that accounts of out-of-body experience [OBE] can be found throughout history. "You can go into Egyptian tombs and see diagrams on the walls of how it's supposed to be done. Greek mystic religions apparently had techniques to induce this experience that were the crux of their initiation ceremonies," Dr. Tart said. "It [OBE] seems to be an altered state of consciousness, which is my principal area of research.

"In the Western world we've rejected these states, we deny they exist when in fact we should be asking such things as, 'Is ESP an evolutionary factor just coming in or just dying out?' And yet in other cultures—all Asia, almost —the altered states of consciousness are acknowledged and used."

Dr. Eugene E. Bernard has studied OBE extensively and has expressed his opinion that it is impossible that so many people who are apparently psychologically healthy might be having hallucinations of traveling in spirit form outside of their physical bodies. "There is still much we don't know about the mind and its abilities," Dr. Bernard has said. "I don't know how long it will take, but I believe that [out-of-body experience] can be proved and controlled."

The great psychical researcher Frederic W. H. Meyers saw out-of-body experience as the manifestation of that which was deepest and most unitary in man's whole being. Of all vital phenomena, Dr. Meyers considered OBE the most significant, ". . . the one definite act which it seems as though a man might perform equally well before and after bodily death."

The numerous accounts of spontaneous out-of-body experience and the carefully conducted experiments in controlled mind projection seem to demonstrate that the human psyche can circumvent the physical limitations of time and space. Although our physical bodies may have to exist in a material world wherein the confining strictures of mass, energy, space, and time shape our environment, it appears that an ethereal part of ourselves, our essential selves, are fully capable of traveling free of our physical bodies.

As in the case of an apparition seen of a loved one at the moment of his death, a spontaneous out-of-body experience seems more likely to occur during a time of crisis or deep emotion, when the normal channels of communication are blocked or removed from either the agent or the recipient of the manifestation. Another factor which both phenomena have in common is that the recipient, who in the case of an OBE may be unaware of the visitation, is usually someone intimately associated with the agent and with whom he shares a bond of love.

"I thought I was dead that night when that automobile struck mine at the intersection," Ernest Mundo writes. "What seemed to be the real me was somewhere above the wreck looking down at all the confusion. I saw the police and a crowd arrive, and I could see my bleeding body slumped forward on the steering wheel. This is it, I thought, I'm dead.

"I wanted to see Laura one last time. I had only to form the thought and I was there, watching her fix dinner, completely unaware of either the accident or my soul there behind her.

"I thought of our only son, who lived in Phoenix. In an instant I was bobbing above him as he sat at his desk in an office.

"I felt no sorrow at leaving them, but I was thankful I had been given the opportunity to see them one last time.

"Then I seemed to feel a tugging and a pulling, and I was being sucked back in a brilliant, swirling blur of color and light. I landed in my body with a jerk, and I heard a voice say, 'Jeez, doc, what's in that needle? It really snapped him back to life.' I heard another man chuckle, and I opened my eyes to see what appeared to be dozens of people pressing forward. I caught a glimpse of the back of a police officer herding the curiosity-seekers back from my automobile; then a sickening rush of pain caused me to lapse back into unconsciousness. This time there was no journey, and I awakened several hours later in a hospital bed with my wife holding my hand."

The *Journal* of the Society for Psychical Research, Vol. XXXII, 1942, carries the account of a Dr. L., a physician who lived at Northampton in England. His wife had gone to Reading, approximately fifty-five miles away, to pay a brief visit to her sister, who was convalescing from an operation. Dr. L. had been unable to leave his practice, so he remained at home.

On July 28, 1942, the doctor reports that although he lay in light sleep, he was conscious of outside noises. "During the night," he states, "I became aware of my wife standing at the side of the bed, near the foot, gently rousing me with her hand on my lower limbs and speaking in a low voice." Dr. L. was certain that he could see his wife standing on the side next to the windows, which were open, and the moonlight made her figure "dim but unmistakable." Mrs. L.'s tone of voice gave the doctor the impression that she was concerned about him.

"She asked if I had minded her going to Reading and leaving me behind," Dr. L. notes. "I assured her that I did not mind at all. She made as if to go away, and I asked her to wait, but she disappeared, though I have no recollection of the manner of her exit."

Dr. L. awakened to find himself staring out the window, and it struck him as peculiar that he had not experienced any awakening from sleep subsequent to his conversation with his wife, only just before, when he had been aroused by the movement of her hand. Dr. L. lay for some time reflecting upon the incident; then he decided to write the next day to ask his wife if she might have had any "untoward" experience on that night.

On Thursday morning [July 30], Dr. L. received a telegram from his wife, which asked: "Are you well?"

On Thursday afternoon Mrs. L. read her husband's letter, which inquired whether or not she had had "any adventures of the mind" on July 28. "If you had any experience at the same time," Dr. L. explained, "it is worth recording and comparing notes."

On July 31 Dr. L. received a reply to his letter of inquiry which related in detail his wife's experiences on the evenings of July 28 and 29. On July 28 she, too, had been sleeping restlessly. She had a great desire to leave her sister's home and to speak with her husband. She went to sleep reflecting that if she were to see her husband that night, she would have to have the ability to fly over the rooftops. Her last persistent thought in the conscious state was that if she could fly like her sister's pet magpie, her troubles would be solved. Although she had no recollection of any dream that corresponded to her husband's experience, the image of her which Dr. L. had seen manifest itself in their home was coincident with the time in which she was drifting off to sleep and wishing that she might see him.

In a statement prepared for the Society for Psychical Research, Mrs. L. went on to testify that the following night, July 29, she dreamed that she had seen her husband standing at the door before her bed. "His figure was ghostly and without definition," she said, "but a shaft of silvery light . . . lit up his features. He was smiling slightly, and there was tenderness in his expression. We did not speak to each other at all. After what seemed a minute or two, his face and figure faded away. . . ."

Mrs. L. interpreted the vision to be an answer to her concern over the husband she had left alone at home. When she recounted her experience the next morning [July 30] at breakfast, however, her son suggested that they send a wire home to see if Father were in good health, so they telegraphed: "Are you well?"

"On Thursday afternoon came a letter from my husband telling me of his experience on the previous Tuesday night," Mrs. L. concluded. "Nothing out of the way occurred after this, and I returned home on August 1."

Many readers will have noticed that a high percentage of the experiences reported in this book have occurred during the hypnagogic state of consciousness which lies between waking and sleeping. It seems that when the conscious mind has relinquished most, but not quite all, of its control over the personality, the unconscious is able to reach out to "tune in" to the true totality of the cosmos. A similar altered state of consciousness exists during hypnotic trance, which may indicate that out-of-body experience may be controlled by certain talented people in somewhat the same manner that telepathy, clairvoyance, and precognition seem to be mentally domesticated by men and women whom we call "psychic sensitives."

Many of those scientific researchers who have been spe-

cializing in the investigation of OBE claims have discovered
men and women whom they have termed "old pros" in
getting in and out of their bodies, seemingly at will. With
sex ranking near the very top of the list of man's basic
drives, it should not really surprise anyone to learn that
certain individuals who have attained "old-pro" proficiency
at controlled OBE have sought to utilize this ability to accomplish sexual activity with loved ones from whom they
were separated. In an earlier book, *Sex and the Supernatural,* I recounted the claims of a number of men and
women who professed to have actually accomplished out-
of-body sexual intercourse. Since the publication of that
book, I have received numerous accounts from others who
offer their personal testimonies that such out-of-body co-
habitation is possible.

"Since both Rachael and I were married to others, it
was virtually impossible to get together except sometimes
very briefly after our class in psychic development," Burt
Phillips told me. "We soon got tired of quickies in the back
seat of my car, so we decided to get together out of the
body. I'd been able to flip out since I was a kid, and Rachael was getting better and better at astral projection.

"We decided to set aside a certain time each night, you
know, when we would be able to be alone to concentrate
on each other and on projecting to each other. We agreed
that since I was more skilled at astral projection, I would
come to her in the astral body and she would concentrate
on making her body receptive to my astral self.

"Man, it worked! And we kept it up for a long time.
Yes, I mean we got actual physical satisfaction. Most of
the time we came together in mutual climax. It was better
than physical intercourse, where you might be distracted by
a dozen different things. This was real intimacy of the mind
as well as the body."

Burt told me that their out-of-body affair terminated after Rachael complained of other entities being attracted
to her sex organs at inconvenient and disturbing times of

the day. "There are certain dangers involved in all of these occult practices," Burt admitted. "While Rachael was lying there opening up her psyche to receive me, she was also broadcasting her receptivity to a whole host of elementals and so forth, who will jump on a mortal woman any chance they get."

I asked a medium what she thought of Rachael's and Burt's out-of-body love affair. She snorted and dismissed their claims in a deprecating tone. "I think they were entering into a telepathic connection during their period of mutual meditation, and this, in turn, was bringing about a kind of psychic mutual masturbation."

Then, with Burt and Rachael summarily categorized as gullible and frustrated lovers, the medium proceeded to tell me of her own sexual encounters on the astral plane. There exists an undercurrent of jealousy among many psychics, not unlike that which exists among professional entertainers. They are always pleased by another's success in the field, and yet, in spite of their good wishes and their striving for high levels of spirituality, they cannot always resist interpreting another's accomplishments as a reminder of their own deficiencies in a certain area.

The tabloid *Midnight* carried an article entitled "Girl Makes Love by ESP" in their March 10, 1969, issue. Although I can make no claims for the piece, which was by-lined Ryan Master, "a psychologist at Oxford University in England," it contains a description of the phenomenon of out-of-body sex which is remarkably similar to that which has been told me by those occult practitioners who profess such abilities.

According to Ryan Master, Angela Fiorelli, a twenty-three-year-old schoolteacher from Nice, France, can make "violent, ecstatic, totally satisfying love to any man she wants" by what would appear to be either mental telepathy or out-of-body projection. The psychologist writes that Miss Fiorelli has only to sit alone in a dimly lighted room, relax, concentrate on the man she wishes to have as a lover, then permit her sexual desires to run rampant. ". . . In a matter of minutes, both she and her mental lover are enjoying all the pleasures of sexual intercourse—up to and including an explosive mutual climax—without any actual physical contact."

Psychologist Masters tells us that he simply ignored the first letters which came to him from Miss Fiorelli, inviting him to investigate her highly unorthodox experiments in ESP. When he finally received a whole packet of letters from men who attested to her extraordinary psychic abilities, Masters decided that he could no longer ignore such evidence.

Masters describes the experiment which he held in the home of Angela Fiorelli's parents in Nice. They occupied separate rooms. He sat at a table, fully clothed, studying some papers which he had brought with him. Angela sat alone in her bedroom.

The psychologist was deeply engrossed in his work; then, suddenly, he found himself in a "fever of sexual excitement." But he insists he was not daydreaming or indulging in erotic fantasy; "this was the real thing."

According to his statement: "I could actually see Angela's face in front of me. I could feel her lips brushing against my cheek, her teeth nibbling at my ear, her hot sweet breath and pointed little tongue entering my mouth."

At this point, it would be unfair to inquire about the psychologist's scientific objectivity. As it is, Masters confesses that he left his desk, undressed, and lay naked on the bed in the room. "As far as I was concerned," he writes, "I had a flesh-and-blood woman in my arms."

After admitting to the observance of tender preliminaries and foreplay, Masters declares a "long, breathtaking period of enjoying the deepest pleasures of each other's body" and a "fantastic mutual climax that bordered on the edge of insanity."

Masters concludes his article by stating that Angela Fiorelli has consented to travel to a parapsychology laboratory and submit to a series of tests designed to determine "how and why her mind works as it does." If the whole piece was not simply fiction passed off as reportage, the laboratory's assessment of the young woman should make for interesting reading, as well as making an important contribution to the literature of psychical research.

Judging by the picture of "Angela" which accompanied the article, one finds it difficult to imagine a young woman of such stunning physical attributes remaining contented with mental exercises, no matter how satisfying they might be. If Angela's claims should be more than fantasy, however, then one might consider that the young woman has achieved a communion of spirit which, if properly controlled, would surely add an enviable bonus to any sexual relationship.

To those who practice the occult arts, out-of-body sexual experience is not all that uncommon, and if the occultist's testimonies are to believed, men and women with talents similar to the alleged abilities of Angela Fiorelli are no more unique than accomplished pianists.

"Whenever a talent, call it power if you will, such as this exists," an occultist told me not long ago," there will always be those who try to subvert it for their own selfish purposes. When people refer to 'black magic,' they are really speaking of ways of imposing one's will upon natural forces, and such talents, like the ability to fire a rifle, can be used for either good purposes or bad.

"One night when I was out of my body during meditation, I suddenly felt myself being pulled in a certain direction, as if I were being sucked into a vortex. At first I became alarmed, but I seemed to hear a voice telling me that I was being taken somewhere for a test.

"Then I was in a bedroom. A young girl lay on the bed. I caught a movement and saw the shadowy figure of a man approaching her bedside. At first I thought that I was witnessing a thief breaking into a home, but then I realized that the whole situation was much more insidious than that. I saw that the other man was also out of the body, and I was given to understand why he had come to this young woman's bedroom.

"The girl tossed fitfully in her bed. A small whimper escaped her lips as the form of the man hovered over her. I knew that this black magician had visited her before, that he had invaded her unconscious mind as she lay sleeping, and had worked his lust upon her innocent body.

"The sleeping victim tossed off her covers, as if she had suddenly grown too warm. The black magician hung there above her like a dark cloud, and I was aware of the mental impressions with which he was bombarding his prey. The girl moaned, as if trying to resist the images flooding her unconscious, but the black magician was clever, a master at manipulating someone who lay in the dream state. She sighed, lifted her nightgown. She was naked beneath the gown, and she opened her thighs to receive her unseen exploiter.

"That was when I moved to his side. He became aware of me at once and swung about, perturbed and defensive, like a hungry wolf prepared to fight for its conquered prey.

"I did not know if I were quite up to doing psychic combat with a black magician of his obvious prowess, but somehow I did not feel foolhardy. I felt as though other forces stood by to aid me. When I saw the fear in his eyes, I knew that I had been correct. Glancing behind me, I saw the images of three etheric masters, or guides, each of whom held flaming swords in their hands. The black magician beat a hasty retreat, leaving his victim to awaken wide-eyed and trembling, as if she had just emerged from a terrible nightmare. At the same time, I felt a tugging at my astral self, and I knew that I was being pulled back to my physical body. I was pleased that I had been able to serve and assist the white brotherhood in combating one who had succumbed to the power of evil."

A highly respected Chicago medium told me of an instance wherein he had become involved with lusty out-of-body projections on an unconscious level, projections which violated his conscious code of ethics.

"L. I. first came to my attention in mid-1967 when our office had a typewriter repaired at the company where she was employed. L. I. was a dark beauty of Spanish and Indian ancestry. She was thirty-five years old, divorced, the mother of two boys, eleven and five. L. I. did not make friends easily. She was devoted to a boyfriend named Pete, an independent truck driver who usually arrived in town once a week and visited her at her mid-Northside home. Pete was still married to another, and his relationship with L. I. might best have been described as 'indefinite.'

"L. I. and I had gotten around to a discussion of ESP and its current popularity. We had become fast friends. I told her about my dream to bring spiritual realization to the Chicago area by setting up a camp similar to the one in Camp Chesterfield, Indiana.

"Fascinated by mysticism, L. I. said that she had been seeking something elusive all her life, and now she felt that she had found it. She told me how she had been close to another man while she was still married. This man, Randy, had been a painter and a mystic. She had last heard from him in the mid-1950's, when he had sent her a strange message: 'The jaws of the Minotaur are closing.'

"I told L. I. of the legend of the dragon beast called the Minotaur that could only be placated by being fed the living bodies of young men. I also mentioned the recent excavations which revealed that such a labyrinth as the one described as the Minotaur's lair really existed.

"L. I. said that she had visited Randy's apartment on several occasions to meditate. She claimed that she had never had sexual relations with the painter there, but that he had made several paintings of her and her children. She pointed to the north wall of her living room, where there hung a portrait of her children which had been done by

Randy. On the west wall there was a huge portrait of a demonlike figure which I knew could only be, and was, Randy. Psychically, I knew that Randy was in spirit.

"We proceeded with L. I.'s development and made arrangements for her enrollment in a spiritual unfoldment class conducted by H. S. at her home on Chicago's mid-Southside.

"Then things began to happen. The spirit form of Randy showed up at the class, appearing first to me, then to others, with his thumb and fingers to his nose in a filthy gesture of contempt. We were all puzzled by such behavior on his part. L. I., obviously upset, said she would speak quietly to Randy in an attempt to calm him. Later, two mediums of our camp, A. F. and M. S., said that they had seen the horns of a demon hovering over me during a midday luncheon meeting.

"An appointment was made with M. S. of Villa Park to give L. I. a reading. M. S. is a medium of high ability who is capable of holding an audible two-way conversation with the spirit guides of the subjects for whom she is reading.

"During the reading, M. S. stated immediately that L. I. was being agitated almost nightly by some outside entity. L. I. agreed and admitted that she frequently went to work feeling as tired as if she had been up all night. M. S. stated flatly that a spirit entity was sexually debauching L. I. night after night, leaving her exhausted by daybreak.

"L. I. was given several predictions of her future by M. S., and she was urged to protect herself from evil by maintaining a small blue light at night and by depositing a scattering of salt in each corner of her bedroom.

"Several days later, I realized that I had not heard from L. I. since her reading session with M. S. Since we had been in almost daily contact, I felt something had happened to disturb our friendship. I knew of nothing that could have caused this, but on a hunch, I decided to call M. S. I was astonished to hear her say: 'It was *you* who was visiting L. I. nightly and forcing sex relations on her!'

"I stammered something about that being impossible. I was not conscious of having been anywhere other than my own bedroom at night, and that was some twenty-five miles away from L. I.'s home.

"After I had questioned M. S. further, I became convinced that I must have become involved in something outside my awareness. M. S. was an experienced adept, and I had never known her to make a false analysis or a careless jest."

The medium, who is a healthy, virile male, admitted to me that if such a beauty as L. I. had given her consent to a sexual liaison, it might have been another matter. "But I am puzzled as to how I came to be identified as the materialized being who was guilty of committing astral rape," he said.

Since I know this medium as a man who would not willingly violate such occult dicta as those strictures against trespassing upon another's free will, I have wondered if the apparently malignant entity known as Randy might not either have masqueraded as the medium or somehow manipulated the medium's astral body to accomplish his own perverse gratification.

Mrs. M. A. H. had no occult terminology to explain what happened to her shortly after her husband's death a few weeks after Christmas in 1939.

"We had been so busy preparing for our wedding date that we had not taken the time to transfer our insurance policies," she writes. "We just assumed that there would be plenty of time after we were married, but just seven weeks after our marriage, my husband died. His mother collected on his two large policies."

To add to Mrs. M. A. H.'s sorrow and confusion, her husband's mother seemed to give no indication whether or not she would contribute any of the money from the policies to the funeral expenses.

Mrs. M. A. H. spent the night after her husband's funeral with her sister. The next morning at dawn, she lay in that mysterious zone of semiconsciousness between wakefulness and sleep. Her husband appeared, took her by the hand, and lifted her out of her body. Mrs. M. A. H. had little time to analyze her emotions during such a bizarre experience, for she was too busy trying to deal with the wonder of it all.

Then they were standing on the porch of their home. Her husband pointed to a small black briefcase which lay on the second of three steps leading to the sidewalk. He smiled, then disappeared, and Mrs. M. A. H. was back in the spare bedroom at her sister's house.

Although she had never seen her husband with such a briefcase, Mrs. M. A. H. could not forget the vision, and she began to search for it. "In the second of the three drawers of my husband's dresser I found it," she said [it is interesting to note how the imagery of the second of three steps represented the second of three drawers]. Inside the briefcase Mrs. M. A. H. found an insurance policy that named no beneficiary. The attached premium book indicated that no premium had been paid for five years, but Mrs. M. A. H. was convinced that the policy was valid.

"I took it immediately to the president of the branch office of the insurance company in our city," Mrs. M. A. H. states, "and within three days I received a substantial check which included interest from the day the policy was issued. I had enough money to pay for the funeral, plus enough extra to get me back on my feet financially. I was told that if my husband had passed away even a few days later, the policy would have been void."

Paul Twitchell, that enigmatic figure who espouses Eckankar, the ancient science of soul travel, told me of another incident wherein two souls, one living, one "dead," met out of the body to bring about a resolution of a weighty problem. In this case, Paul Twitchell's stepsister had to convince a restless spirit that it was no longer among the living.

The incident occurred during Twitchell's first visit to Paris, when he was in his teens. He had been graduated from high school, and his foster grandmother had financed his trip as a reward for his finishing school with good grades. Besides, the crafty old woman had wanted a first-hand report on Paul's stepsister, Katie, who was studying art in the City of Light.

"Sri Sudar Singh, the first living master of Eckankar, was in Paris on a Western tour," Twitchell recalls. "He was giving lectures in a hall near the Place de la Concorde. We went to hear him one night, and it was one of the few times that we took a cab. Generally, due to our financial condition, we rode a bus or pedaled our bicycles.

"On this particular night it was raining slightly, and wisps of fog hung over the Seine and the streets of Paris. It was a long way to Montmartre, where Katie lived. It was a night for ghosts, and it was a ghost that we encountered. I have never forgotten that experience, for it gave me a knowledge of the astral body of man, which may, on occasion, wander about forlornly in old haunts, trying to make contact with former friends and people still in the flesh.

"Since then I have had much experience with so-called ghosts. Some I have exorcised; some I have taken to their rightful place in the other worlds; and others I have put in the hands of the heavenly helpers to be taken care of like children.

"We finally caught a cab on the Avenue Gabriel. When Katie told the driver in French where we were going, he spoke with rapid gestures.

"I was surprised at the argument which developed between them. Katie informed me that he wanted our fare, which was on the hill behind the Sacre Coeur Cathedral, but he didn't want to take the usual route, for it passed a cemetery. She knew he was afraid, but she couldn't understand why. They threw words at each other for the next few minutes; then she settled back in the seat and told me this story.

" 'He says he doesn't want to pass a certain cemetery which is on the way to our flat. His reason is that two years ago on a rainy night such as this he picked up a man standing under a tree near the graveyard about this time of night.

" 'The fare gave him the name of a café in the area. He didn't pay much attention to his customer but drove on with his thoughts on a fight he had had with his wife before leaving his home that night. When he got to the café and stopped for the fare to get out and pay, the man had disappeared.

" 'It unnerved him so that he quit for the night and went home. It tormented him so badly that next day he drove to the café and looked up the proprietor.

" 'The cafe owner said the cabbie's fare had been the ghost of a man who had been killed by a jealous husband over the latter's wife.

" 'The lovers had been using his café as a rendezvous, for the café was somewhat off the beaten track. The husband found out about the lover, and one night, when it was rainy like tonight, followed them there and shot the man when the two were leaving the café. The girl escaped unharmed. The slain lover was buried in the cemetery where the cab has to pass.

" 'Other cab drivers have had similar experiences with the ghostly lover, who seems to be wanting to get back to the café, where he hopes the girl still awaits him. Nobody wants to pass that particular spot, especially on a rainy night.'

"At last Katie talked the driver into passing the old graveyard, with the promise that she wouldn't allow any harm to come to him. It was a hard task to convince him, but somehow she had done it.

"My nerves were on edge. I had many times seen and

talked with entities on the other side of the veil of death, including some of the masters of Eckankar, but nothing in my youthful experience had quite prepared me for such an encounter with a restless spirit.

"The rain had turned into a light mist when we reached the place where the ghost was supposed to be. There was a corner with some shrubbery, dimly lighted by an old street-lamp, just the place for a ghost. The driver almost went into hysterics. My heart jumped. Under the streetlamp was a figure outlined in the misting rain, its hand up trying to hail the cab.

" 'Stop and pick him up,' Katie ordered in French.

"With a deep moan of fear the driver skidded to a stop. A deep, penetrating coldness entered the cab as the door swung open. A dark figure with gloomy face and fearful eyes got in and sat down on the other side of my stepsister. In a deep, ghoulish voice, it gave the address of the café.

"Katie began to talk. I didn't understand what she was saying, mainly because of my shaken nerves. But it sound-ed like a low, frightful hum, which was answered in the same manner and tone.

"Katie ordered the cab to halt and wait until she was through with the rites of exorcising the ghost. Suddenly I noticed that she was outside herself in her Nuri-Sarup body, the light-body, and that her physical self was slumped as if it were asleep.

"Then within the wink of an eye, she wasn't there any-more, and neither was the ghost. She had gone to take him back into that world from which he had come. I was able to watch her through the secret methods of being above the body, taught by the Eckankar masters.

"She took him into the astral world, where an entity, dressed in the fashion of a nun, whose shining face was ex-traordinarily beautiful, met them. She took the distressed one from Katie, blessed her, and promised to take care of him.

"My stepsister returned immediately to her body in the

car. She opened her physical eyes and acted as if aroused from a deep sleep.

"She told the cabbie to drive on. 'Nobody will be bothered by him again,' she said matter-of-factly.

"I learned the method of exorcising ghostly intruders from her that night. I have since determined that the ghostly lover never again returned to its old haunts."

14. GHOSTLY VISIONS
OF LIVING LOVERS

Another category of phenomena which must surely be linked to out-of-body journeys of the spirit, and, indeed, may be but *unconscious* astral projections, are those instances in which men and women have been confronted with the apparitions of loved ones who still solidly reside within their fleshly shells.

One evening Gordon North had worked late. It was nearly ten o'clock before he returned home. There were few lights left on in his house, but as he opened the door, he thought he caught a glimpse of Karen, his wife of three months, hiding in a corner of the front room.

Believing the playful Karen sought to tease him, Gordon pretended not to see her, then suddenly whirled toward the spot where she crouched behind a piece of furniture. Karen managed to evade him, and she danced lightly out of the reach of his arms. Gordon pursued his wife about the room, but she moved always just out of his grasp.

At last Gordon darted forward and laughingly cornered his wife by the wall. He gave a shout of triumph, but as he was about to throw his arms around her, he heard a peculiar sound, like a report of a faraway rifle, and Karen vanished before his astonished eyes.

He stepped back from the wall, his brain literally throbbing in an effort to classify the incident he had just witnessed.

"Gordon, what on earth are you doing out in the living room?" It was Karen's voice coming from the bedroom. "What is all that noise?"

Gordon North found his wife in bed, where she insisted she had been all the time, having grown weary of waiting up for him.

Mrs. T. B. C. saw her husband's double one night as he lay sleeping beside her.

"I was sleeping very restlessly that night," she remembers. "We had gone to bed too early, really, and now it was only a little past midnight, and I had awakened. As I turned my head toward my husband, I saw a most remarkable thing. Jim's astral body, or soul, was rising out of his physical body. It sat up beside him for a moment; then it got up and walked toward the bathroom door.

"I knew that I was wide awake, and I was just a little frightened. 'Where are you going, Jim?' I called after the astral Jim, but, of course, it paid no attention to me. The physical Jim still lay sleeping peacefully beside me. The astral body of my husband stood before the bathroom door, as if undecided whether or not it should leave the bedroom.

"I was able to get a good look at Jim's astral body as it walked across the room. It was identical to Jim's physical body, red hair, same pajamas, everything. His astral body, though, had a silver glow around it, and it was transparent. I could see Jim's soul distinctly, and yet I could see through it."

Mrs. T. B. C. closed her eyes for a few moments and prayed that all was well with her husband. When she opened her eyes again, Jim's soul body had returned to his physical shell, and her husband lay sleeping restfully beside her.

The experience convinced Mrs. T. B. C. that it is possible for the soul of man to exist outside of his body while the physical body lies in sleep or in trance. She also believes that the incident provided her with proof that the soul of man goes on living after the death of the physical body.

In the November, 1965, issue of *Fate* magazine, Albert Keltner related a remarkable experience which told of how he and his vanished sweetheart were reunited through the efforts of her astral double.

Myrtle Thayer had disappeared on March 17, 1959, leaving Keltner totally despondent. He describes himself as existing in a kind of "robotized consciousness," desperately trying to find something to occupy his mind.

Sometimes when he would sit in his room, staring at nothing, a mistlike form would appear which would gradually assume the physical proportions of his lost girl friend. It would remain motionless for a few seconds, then disappear. After several materializations, Keltner spoke to the misty form in a voice as pleasant and soothing as he could manage under the circumstances.

"As we became better acquainted," Keltner writes, "it began to extend its visits. I would say, 'Hello, dear. . . . You are a woman, aren't you?' The head would nod slowly. It never spoke audibly, only by signs or movements."

After numerous visitations, Keltner discovered that he could communicate telepathically with his ethereal friend. "Do you know where my sweetheart is?" he asked the entity.

"Immediately the form answered, 'Yes, I am she. I was in a car accident the evening I left you. I'm in a hospital, alive but unconscious. Stay where you are. I'll find you. Wait! I can't remember clearly; my body must be healed again. It will take a while; I don't know how long, for my neck is broken.'"

Keltner wanted to know if there was not something that

he could do to help her. He explained that he had already contacted the missing-persons bureau, with no results. He wanted to know a dozen things, such as the name of the hospital in which her unconscious body lay.

The misty white form told him that there was nothing that he could do to help her now. "I will come to you again when I'm feeling better," she said.

Albert Keltner waited another week, a month, a year, but the image of his sweetheart did not reappear. Perhaps the astral body had only wished to make contact, to let him know that she still lived in the physical body, but we can imagine the thoughts that must have gone through Keltner's confused brain. He must have wondered if that misty form had really been that of his love, and if it had been, was she now dead, since she no longer appeared to him? Keltner writes that he tried to forget his "misty maiden," but he remained single, haunted by her plea that he wait for her.

On the morning of July 3, 1964, more than five years after Mrytle Thayer had disappeared, the smoky, transparent image of a woman once again appeared to Keltner as he sat relaxing in an easy chair. When Keltner expressed his concern over her long absence, the entity replied that nothing bad had happened. "It will take only a short while now, for my body is almost healed. If you will go to the local laundromat on August 2, there will be a bigger surprise for you."

Keltner resolved to keep the appointment. On the second day of August, he collected his soiled laundry and went to the laundromat. He had just selected a machine and had begun to place his clothes into it when he heard a familiar voice behind him. He turned in amazement to see the sweetheart whom he had not seen in the physical body for so many years.

Once they had recovered from their astonishment in having accomplished such a miraculous meeting, Myrtle explained her disappearance.

The day she left Albert, she had become involved in a five-car collision which had been caused by a loaded gravel truck that had gone out of control. The runaway truck had tipped over on Myrtle's car and demolished it. Her neck had been broken and her memory impaired. As she lay there unconscious, her astral double had appeared to Keltner in his apartment. Later, as the years passed, Myrtle had regained consciousness, but her damaged memory prevented her from remembering the name of her beloved. Shortly before her release from the hospital, she had once again contacted Albert in her astral body and arranged the rendezvous in the laundromat. Although her memory could not provide her with Albert's name, Myrtle's essential self did not have to bother with such physical handicaps. Her astral body could transcend time and space and simply be there before the sweetheart who had promised to wait.

There are cases reported in which the astral double of a loved one has brought a forewarning of danger or has managed to interact with an individual in such a manner as to save his life.

Martha Pilgrim (née Hyland) remembers her father as a great sportsman, a man who loved to be the first hunter into the field whenever a new season opened. Martha's mother had no objections to her husband's pleasure in hunting, but she did object quite strongly to the fact that he and his friends would stop by a particular bar and grill for an early breakfast so that they might lace their morning coffee with some Irish whiskey.

"I was thirteen that season," Martha writes, "and I can remember Pop noisily assembling all his gear to join his friends at Tony's grill. Mom just stayed in bed, because she knew Pop wouldn't be eating breakfast before he left. Since Pop had made so much racket, I decided that I m ght as well get up and get my homework out of the way for the weekend. I thought that if I got all my work done,

Mom might reverse her decision and allow me to go to the matinee that day.

"I had finished breakfast and was working at the kitchen table when Pop stormed into the house, livid with rage. I had never seen him so angry.

" 'Where's your mother!' he yelled at me. 'Never has she done so foul a thing to me!'

"I told Pop that Mom was still in bed, and he moved over to me as if he were going to strike me. 'So now she has you doing her lying for her, too, eh? Have I got back to the house before her?'

"I insisted that Mom lay in her bed and told Pop to go look. The keys for our second car hung on their hook beside the kitchen door. Neither of us had left the house for even a minute.

"What with Pop banging his fist on the table and stomping around in the kitchen, it was not long before Mom came out of the bedroom to see what was the matter. She stood in the doorway of the kitchen, fastening her bathrobe and stifling a yawn. All the color just kind of drained out of Pop's face. It was obvious even to a man as angry as he that Mom was just getting up. He poured himself a cup of coffee and drank it with shaking hands. Then he told us what had happened to him that morning.

" 'I was sitting in Tony's with the fellows, when I saw Mom sitting across the room. She was the only woman in the bar, and it was crowded with hunters. I felt embarrassed, and the fellows at our booth started teasing me about the "old lady checking up on me." Every time I'd try to catch Mom's eye, she would smile and turn away from me, like she was pretending not to see me.

" 'Finally I got up from the table and went over to her and asked her just what she was trying to do to me. But she wouldn't answer. She just smiled and got up and walked out of the bar. The fellows started gouging me about how henpecked I was, how I couldn't even stop by for some Irish coffee without my wife checking up on me.

I got so mad I told them I was going to follow Mom home and find out just what her big idea had been.

" 'But now,' he sighed, 'I find that you've never been out of bed.' Pop slumped forward in his chair, took his head between his hands. 'Am I losing my mind?'

"Mom told him that it must have been some other woman, but Pop answered that he should know his own wife after living with her for sixteen years. Pop was convinced that he had been given some strange omen, and he decided not to rejoin his friends. He called Tony's grill, but found out that they had already left without him and had told the bartender where Pop could locate them."

Martha remembers that her father accompanied her to the matinee that day, one of the few times that the two of them had ever attended a motion picture together. They stopped after the picture and had some ice cream, and Martha felt a closeness to her father that she had not experienced for some time. Her father even joked about that morning. He confessed to his daughter that he probably would have drunk too much if he had gone with the men.

When they returned home that afternoon, Martha and her father found her mother sitting on the sofa weeping. She had just heard on the local news that all of Pop's hunting companions had been killed in a head-on collision as they had been returning home.

"Pop always felt that he had been spared for some reason," Martha Pilgrim states. "He believed that it must have been his guardian angel that had assumed Mom's shape on that morning in order to keep him home and out of that death car."

The astral double of a stranger prevented Phyllis Schneider from giving herself to a man who would have caused her only heartache and sorrow.

"Spencer literally swept me off my feet," Miss Schneider admitted in her account of her strange experience. "I was not yet twenty and very inexperienced in the ways of love.

Spencer was eight years older than I, and he seemed to be the very epitome of masculine charm and strength."

Phyllis was even more pleased when her parents also warmed to her beau. Spencer revealed that he was an avid fisherman, a passion shared by the entire Schneider family, and soon the young man became a part of their family outings. By midsummer Spencer and Phyllis were at the "engaged-to-be-engaged" period of their courtship.

Spencer and Phyllis had met at a dance, and since Spencer lived in another city quite some distance from Phyllis, he had to drive several miles to see her. Because of the problem of the mileage which separated them, they seldom saw each other during the week, but after Spencer had ingratiated himself to Phyllis' parents, he often stayed the weekend with the Schneiders.

One Thursday night before he was coming to stay with them, Spencer called to ask Phyllis if her parents would mind keeping a trunk of his personal possessions in the attic storeroom. "That way," he explained, "I'll always have shirts and ties and a toothbrush available, and I won't have to be hauling so much stuff back and forth with me." Such a plan seemed to make good sense to the Schneiders, and permission was readily granted.

By late summer, however, Phyllis was beginning to have vague feelings of discomfort and concern in regard to her persistent suitor.

One night as they were parked beside a lake, she felt herself about to give an affirmative answer to the Big Question. Spencer's hands had been roaming her body with gentle insistence, his fingers expertly probing and touching sensitive areas. The combination of his mouth on her own and the steady, sensual pressure of his fingers had kindled a fire within her that Phyllis knew could only be extinguished by the act of physical love. She had always vowed that she would wait until she had a wedding band around her finger before she allowed any man to claim her virginity, but Spencer had already unbuttoned her blouse without meeting any resistance from her. The fingers of one hand were tugging at the hook of her bra, while the fingers of his other hand were at the zipper of her slacks.

That was when Phyllis called a halt to the proceedings. Spencer was just too damned experienced. "Spencer," she asked him, "have you had a lot of women before me?"

His only answer was a kind of mirthful gurgle deep in his throat.

"Well, have you ever been married?" she wondered.

Spencer's hands became suddenly inactive. He leaned back against the seat. "Why do you ask?" he asked softly.

"Well, you are nearly twenty-eight," Phyllis said. "People do get married, you know."

She could see his white teeth in the dim illumination from the dashboard. Spencer was smiling at her. Such wonderfully white teeth, she sighed mentally, such a handsome, tanned face, such a . . . Phyllis shook her head. No more of that. She began to button her blouse.

"Of course people get married," Spencer teased. "That's why I want you to marry me."

"But have you ever been married before?"

Spencer did not answer until he had lit a cigarette. "I was married once," he admitted. "I was married to a pretty blond girl who died in childbirth."

"Oh, Spencer," Phyllis said; "I'm sorry." She felt at once ashamed that she had wrung the truth out of him and disappointed that he had not told her about his previous marriage before. "And . . . the child?"

"Peter," he said, expelling the name in a cloud of cigarette smoke, "lives with my mother. He's six years old."

Phyllis swallowed hard. If they married after her birthday in December, she would be a twenty-year-old bride with a six-year-old stepson. Oh, well, he was Spencer's son, and she loved Spencer.

"Peter must come to live with us as soon as we're married," she blurted out.

Spencer grabbed her happily, gave her a long kiss. "Name the date," he said. "Just name the date."

"The night I decided on December sixteenth as our wedding date," Phyllis relates, "I had the most terrible kind of nightmare. When I awakened, I knew that I was not alone in the room. I nearly screamed when I saw a strange woman outlined with a silver light standing at the foot of my bed. I could distinguish no features, and when I sat up to turn on the bedlamp, the ghostly thing vanished."

The next night was a carbon copy of the previous one. First, a strange, frightening nightmare, then the eerily glowing woman at the foot of her bed. Phyllis began to fear that she might be losing her mind.

"On the third night," Phyllis tells in her account, "the same nightmare seized me. I dreamed that I had married Spencer and we had gone away to live in our own home. Then Spencer began to build a cage around me, and I began to scream hysterically. I felt that I was losing my mind. Whenever I would scream too loudly, several nurses would appear from nowhere and tell me to be quiet or they would stick me with their needles. And all the while Spencer kept building the cage around me, until, at last, I saw that it was not a cage at all, but a coffin!

"It was at that point each night that I would awaken. When I awakened on the third night, I heard a voice calling to me. The shimmering image once again stood before me, only this time I could make out features and distinguish long, blond hair flowing down to her shoulders.

"'You must not marry Spencer,' the ghost told me. 'You think you will be his wife, but you will have done wrong. You think I am dead, but I am not. I am not dead. *I am not dead!*'"

Sleep for Phyllis the rest of that night was impossible. She sat up in bed, staring until dawn at the space where the strangely illuminated woman had stood. That morning she told her mother and sisters about her terrible nocturnal experiences of the past three nights.

"Look in his trunk in the attic," declared her fifteen-year-old sister, who read far too many gothic romances; "I'll bet you'll find a key to his terrible secret in that trunk."

Phyllis was surprised when her mother agreed with her youngest daughter. "I know that it is a violation of the ethics which Dad and I have tried to instill in you girls," her mother said, "but it just may be that there might be some kind of clue to Spencer's past in that trunk."

They knew that Spencer kept the key to the trunk with him, but an old family friend who could be trusted to be discreet was an accomplished locksmith.

"In one compartment of the trunk, we found an insurance policy which was still in force for a Mrs. Spencer ———. There was another policy on Spencer which named Mrs. Spencer ——— as the beneficiary. I knew that one does not pay premiums on policies on a deceased wife, nor does one declare a dead woman a beneficiary. Then Mother found a number of receipts which had been paid to a sanatorium in a nearby state. It seemed that Spencer's wife had not died, but rather, had suffered a nervous breakdown after the birth of their son."

Although she knew it would be like turning a knife in her flesh, Phyllis asked her parents to accompany her to the sanatorium so that she might verify the circumstantial evidence with firsthand investigation. "Mom and Dad consented, and we set out on the long drive to the mental hospital. Dad used the pretext that we were old family friends, and we were given permission to visit Spencer's wife. Thank God we had chosen a day when she was enjoying a period relatively free from trauma and delusion.

"I nearly fainted when I saw the woman, for I recognized her at once as the pretty, long-haired blond who had appeared in my room."

The Schneiders chatted with the woman about her husband and son, and Phyllis was grateful that her parents had come along to bear the burden of the conversation. Her father told the woman that Spencer had been very busy and had been working long hard hours, but that he sent his love. "But he hasn't been to see me for so long," the woman said sadly. "Please tell him to come to see me. He . . . he acts like I'm dead."

"My father called Spencer that night when we returned to our home," Phyllis concludes her story. "He told him to come to pick up his trunk and not to see me again. I heard Dad strongly urge him to take a greater interest in the wife and son whom he was shamefully neglecting. Dad later told me that Spencer had become furious with us for meddling in his private life, and he had demanded to know who had told us of his wife in the institution. We had no common friends, and no one among his friends knew that he had been seeing me. Dad simply told him that an interested party who had wanted to keep me from misery and shame had decided to intervene. I guess Dad's way of phrasing it is as good as any."

15. DREAM LOVERS WHO CAME TRUE

For centuries man's love ballads have included a good many melodies whose lyrics tell of dream lovers, who, the songs promise, will one day materialize as lovers of warm and acquiescent flesh. According to some men and women, their real-life experiences substantiate the promises made by those romantic songs and prove that a seed of love planted in a dream can someday produce a mature and lasting relationship. In this chapter we shall explore some case histories of certain individuals who claim to have been haunted by a dream lover for years, until, one day, the very image of their nocturnal mate appeared before them as a very real human being.

Fred A. had his adolescent love life, which in nearly every teen-ager is fraught with emotional storms, further complicated by a vivid dream that he had when he was sixteen.

He had never been far off his parent's farm in Nebraska, but in his dream he was walking along a road that led to an old covered bridge that spanned a small creek. It was a beautiful autumn day, and multicolored leaves lay piled everywhere. As he crossed the bridge, he could see an old stone farmhouse, quite unlike anything that one would find in Nebraska. Boldly he entered the kitchen of the house, where he found a lovely young girl with long blond hair. She was dressed plainly, but she was possessed of a natural beauty that did not require the accentuation of elegant clothing. She smiled at Fred, a warm, loving smile, then began to walk toward him, her softly curving hips moving sensuously under the fabric of her cotton dress.

"Because it was a dream," Fred A. noted with amusement, "she walked right into my outstretched arms. It seemed as though we had known each other for years. We kissed; we hugged; we were delightfully happy in each other's arms. I called her by name, and she whispered my name over and over again.

" 'Don't keep me waiting too long,' she said, becoming anxious when I said that I must go. 'I'll wait as long as I can, but don't keep me waiting too long!' "

The dream left Fred feeling strangely warm and exhilarated. There was a girl waiting for him somewhere. What did pimples on his face and petty quarrels with the girls in his class matter now? Somewhere his true love waited for him.

But, at the same time, Fred felt terribly lonely. Where was the girl now, when he needed her? There were proms and picnics and dances to attend right then.

"I knew that I had to put the dream girl out of my mind," Fred recalled. "I dated a lot of really wonderful girls, but at the oddest and sometimes most inopportune moments, my thoughts flashed back to that beautiful dream image. In my dream I had said her name, but upon awaking, I could remember it only as something like 'Brenda,' but I knew that was not correct."

When World War II broke out, Fred enlisted and was sent overseas to England. "My dream went with me," he stated in an account of his dream lover which he prepared for interested researchers. "I certainly did not lead a monk-like existence, but while my buddies were forming steady relationships and some were taking war brides, I found myself haunted by my dream mate. How often did I argue with myself that I should marry some nice English girl rather than sit alone at night in the canteen, brooding over what may only have been the figment of some fantasy. Certain of my close friends began to wonder what was eating me, but I never dared to tell them. They probably would have had me out on a mental discharge."

Fred was discharged in 1945, and through a mix-up in his papers, found himself stranded in New York City for a few days. A buddy of his from Vermont invited him to spend the weekend at his folks' farm. After nearly four years in London, New York City held no big thrills for him, so Fred decided to accept his friend's offer. He had never seen a New England farm before, and a taste of rural living would help recondition him for Nebraska.

"It was my time for mix-ups, it seemed," Fred continued. "Jim's folks were supposed to pick us up at the bus depot, but when we arrived, there was no one there. Jim had left the message with his seven-year-old brother, and he feared that the word might not have been relayed to his parents. 'It's only a couple of miles out of town.' Jim grinned. 'It's a beautiful day, and it might feel good to stretch our legs after that bus ride. Mind walking?' "

The two ex-soldiers had not hiked far when Fred had the strangest feeling that he had walked along that country road once before. Then they turned a corner, and he saw the old covered bridge that he had seen in that haunting adolescent dream. It was the same kind of startlingly lovely fall day, and the leaves were piled just as he remembered them.

"I knew that around the next bend we would see that old stone farmhouse, but what I had not guessed was that the place would be Jim's home. He led me through the back door into the kitchen. My heart was thudding so hard that I thought I would faint. I knew *she* would be there in the kitchen, and *she* was. An eighteen-year-old girl in a plain cotton housedress turned to smile at us from the sink where she was peeling potatoes. Her long blond hair swirled about her face as she ran to give Jim a warm kiss of welcome. 'Hey, Fred,' Jim laughed, freeing himself from the girl's embrace, 'meet my kid sister, Brenna.' "

So it had been Brenna, not Bren*da*, Fred thought to himself. But he was too tongue-tied to say much of anything. The lovely blond who stood before him, Jim's sister, was the girl of his dream.

"Brenna and I were in love before dinner that night," Fred concluded his account. "I will always remember her first words of love to me: 'Fred, darling, I've waited all my life for you.' Today we are as much in love as we were on our honeymoon, and we have four children as physical proof of our love. I shall never be able to explain that remarkable dream. At the time that I first saw my 'dream girl,' she was only about twelve years old, yet I saw her as vividly as if she had been in the flesh, and just as she appeared on the day that I actually, physically, walked into her life."

Martin J. saw his dream lover when he was in college, and he did not have long to wait before he met her in the wide-awake world.

"I knew my ribs cracked when the two fullbacks from ———— State creamed me," Martin said. "I blacked out, and I saw this pretty black-haired chick standing laughing at me. 'Clumsy,' she laughed. 'You should be more careful. I'm just going to have to look after you.' Then I opened my eyes and saw the coach bending over me. He wasn't nearly as pretty as the chick in my dream, but at least he wasn't laughing at me. A couple of the guys helped me off the field. The crowd yelled a noisy tribute to the fallen gladiator, but I knew that I was one Saturday hero who had been benched for a good while.

"The team doc taped my ribs, but he told me that he wanted me to go to the hospital on Sunday and get X rays, just to be sure. The next day I got this chick I had been going with to drive me out to the hospital. I left her sitting in the car, and I walked kind of cautious-like up the stairs. My ribs hurt.

"I was walking down the hallway to X ray when I saw this really groovy bird in her white nurse's outfit coming toward me. I knew there was something familiar about her, but before my brain could put it all together, I actually walked into a water cooler. The pain in my ribs was terrible, and I fell to the floor. When I looked up, this gorgeous nurse had her hands on her hips and was laughing at me. I almost mouthed the words along with her as it all came back to me. 'Where are you going?' she asked me. I told her, 'X ray, ma'am,' and she laughed again and said, 'Clumsy, you should be more careful. I guess I'll just have to walk along with you and look after you.'

"Later I talked an intern into running out to tell my girl that I had to be held for a while for observation. Ruth, the nurse, and I went out that night, and we plan to be married right after my graduation."

Irene Turnbull Mikolaizyk had been widowed for three years following the death of her husband, James McCliggott, when she decided to leave Saginaw, Michigan, and go to live with her sister in Flint. Although her sister tried her best to make Irene feel welcome, the new widow continued to feel lonely and frustrated. She knew that life should not end for a healthy woman when she was only fifty-one.

One night shortly after her arrival in Flint, Irene had a vivid dream in which she was back in Saginaw, living in a small house. It was a Sunday in her dream, and she was on her way to church. As she passed a gasoline station, she realized that she needed some change for the collection plate. The manager of the station was a friendly, middle-aged man who was glad to accommodate her. They visited a few moments, and Irene learned that his name was

Frank, that he, too, had lost his mate, and that he was a member of the church she was going to attend for the first time. He asked if he might accompany her some Sunday, and Irene expressed her consent to such a plan, adding that he should stop by for a cup of coffee sometime. In her dream, she saw Frank coming to her house, saw them keeping company for a time, then saw them being married in the church in the autumn.

Whether the dream had a contributing factor on Irene's decision to return to Saginaw remains unimportant to her today. On her third trip back, she found just the house for which she had been searching, and within a week she had moved into her new home.

"Come Sunday, I started walking to church," she wrote in the October, 1964, issue of *Fate*. "I got the thought to check my money for the collection, and found that I had to have a bill changed. I went into a gasoline station, and the middle-aged man that made my change seemed strangely familiar to me. His name was Frank Mikolaizyk. Everything worked out exactly like it had in my dream. We were married in the fall when the leaves were coming down. . . ."

A psychic told me of a handsome client of his who had always been extremely popular with the opposite sex, but who had reached the age of thirty-three with his bachelor status intact.

"I used to tease him," the psychic said. "I used to ask him just what he was looking for. I would name each of the girls I had seen him with and enumerate all of their good points. Then I would challenge him to choose one of them for his wife. 'No,' he would tell me, 'Somehow I will know when I have found the right girl. She will be the girl that I once married in a dream.'

"At last, almost overnight it seemed, the rascal got himself married. He called me from a nearby city and told me that he had not needed my psychic impressions about this girl. He had met her while on a business trip and had fallen instantly in love with her. On the second day of their whirlwind courtship, he had said to her, 'I know you. We were married in a dream that I had when I was twenty.' The girl had replied: 'And I know you. I had that same dream when I was fifteen. You were the groom, and I have been searching for you ever since.' "

There will be some who will say that such dreams are the result of the soul's yearning for its true soulmate, whose identity and whereabouts are known to the transcendent level of the unconscious mind. This information somehow manages to bubble up to the conscious mind during that altered state of consciousness which we call dreaming. The image of the soulmate thereby becomes an object of idealized love to the dreamer, and he becomes obsessed with searching for the lover whom he has glimpsed in the shadow world of his dreams. Others will inject elements from the reincarnation hypothesis into accounts of dream lovers come true and will maintain that certain mates must be sought out in order that patterns of karma may be fruitfully played out.

The gifted Chicago psychic Teddy O'Hearn had the following to say about man's search for the divine soulmate:

"Mark this well, there is a great tapestry being woven as each of us entwines our lives with the other in our journey through the earth. This tapestry is, at one and the same time, a record of the past, as well as a means for each thread—each person—to evolve and to reach that perfection in an evolution which will free the individual from earth's tapestry, and the further necessity of returning to its travail. Woven into this tapestry are ugliness, horror, agony, suffering, and tears, as well as beauty, joy, a measure of fulfillment, and happiness. As in all of nature, nothing is ever lost.

". . . Only by experiencing the depths of what is inherent in the lowest can we reach the heights of the mystical ecstasy (union with God and our divinely ordained other half, our soulmate) which transcends beyond imagination anything possible in earthly experience.

"Regardless of the name one bears in any one earth lifetime, each of us has the eternal 'I' which carries either the male or female connotation of the androgynous being which we all were in the beginning, before Adam and Eve.

"The separation of the sexes came at that point in time depicted by the Bible's symbolic story of Adam, wherein God made the androgynous Adam two—male and female, negative and positive, Adam and Eve.

"At this time, earth's beings evolved into self-consciousness. This was *not* a fall from grace, but a further step in human evolution in order that the male and female counterparts of each entity might experience and learn and eventually be reunited when they had evolved through the testing of earth experience and attained the point at which each has earned the right to a reunion with his divine other half. This is the true soulmate, the only 'other' that each of us can look forward to meeting one day. It is with the soulmate that we will share complete fulfillment, a fulfillment beyond anything which we may ever know in any relationship on earth.

"Our conscious mind may have long since forgotten its soulmate, but the soul memory we have of our divine 'other half' filters through, though dimly, to our consciousness and leads us to a constant yearning and searching for complete and loving fulfillment which may continue life after l fe. It is this search which provides us with the means whereby we learn that love is not possession, that love is not self-serving, that love is not tyrannical or cruel, that love is not sex alone in any of its ramifications.

"We learn by trial and error through many loves and many lives, often encountering the same mates over and over again. All of these mates are soulmates by reason of the mutual learn ng process which takes place, but they must not be confused with the divine soulmate, both halves of which are seldom encountered in the physical earth plane. Each of these earthly soulmate relationships must be transmuted, from disharmony to harmony, into true universal love.

". . . We must learn real love through countless lifetimes of giving and receiving, of dealing with imitations and misconceptions of the real thing, of learning to cope with enmity, in order to achieve a complete education in lovemaking which will make us fit for the reunion with the divine soulmate.

"Thus in our searching and learning process we encounter many of the same 'loves' over and over again—sometimes as parents, as sisters, as brothers, as children, as friends, as enemies, as business associates, as teachers, as students, as well as lovers and husbands and wives. Our relationship with any one other individual is a learning experience and a perfection of the many facets of love. When we have learned and earned the right, we will begin to realize that love is indeed universal, rather than personal, that love, tempered by wisdom, is the tool we have to carry with us in our release from our earth lives. When we progress to the next step on the ladder and achieve the reunion and the fulfillment of self in the personal love of our divine soulmate, the two of us, as one, will go on into the fulfillment of ourselves in the work of the Father.

"So you see, we are all of us 'haunted lovers.' Our search for our divine soulmates makes us so."

16. OTHER LIVES, OTHER LOVES

There is, perhaps, no tale quite so romantic as that of reincarnated lovers who once again manage to find each other over the span of centuries. Unfortunately, it seems that the joy in encountering a remembered love is largely relegated to fictional romances. Among those individuals who claim real-life reunions with past loves from other lives, personal anguish, rather than personal happiness, appears to be the most commonly experienced emotion. Although some men and women have entered into happy marital unions as a result of a conviction that they had been sweethearts, lovers, or spouses in a past life, many reincarnated lovers feel that such an awareness of past intimacies with others has miserably complicated their lives with their present-life mates.

"I know that William and I must have a terrible karma to work out," a buyer for a large department store wrote this author. "I am happily married and have been for ten years. Joseph is a very understanding husband, so understanding that he would listen to me explain to him about William."

The woman, whom we shall call Diana, had been haunted by a recurring dream ever since her early adolescence. In the dream she saw herself dying of a fever in a rudely built cabin. A man stood at the foot of her bed, looking down on her with distaste. He seemed afraid, as if she had some dread disease to which he in no way wanted to be exposed. He turned his back to her, walked out the door. Then Diana saw the flames crackling up around her bed.

"At this point I would awaken, screaming my terror and sorrow," she said. "I knew that the man was my husband. I knew that we lived in a crude cabin and that before he deserted me, he set fire to the cabin to destroy both me and my disease."

Diana led an active adolescence and was in no appreciable way inhibited by the dream, which she considered a memory of a past life. She had a morbid fear of fire and was perhaps overly concerned about communicable diseases—she would go to great lengths to avoid contact with anyone who suffered from so mild an affliction as a cold —but such idiosyncrasies would not unduly cripple one's social development. She married soon after her graduation from college, and her union with Joseph soon produced two daughters. Then she met William.

"He was getting off an elevator when I first saw him," Diana said. "His eyes seemed to pierce me to my very essence. I stood as if I had been turned to stone. Those were the eyes I had seen so often in my dream. A strange rush of both love and hatred filled my trembling body. I wanted to kiss him and strike him down at the same time. Somehow I managed to push past him and get into the elevator.

"When I returned to my office, I was shocked to find him waiting for me. I know that I must have paled, and I could not even find the intelligence to ask him his business. He seemed oblivious to my discomfort. He stood, flashed me a professional smile, and introduced himself as the new salesman for one of our largest suppliers.

"I mumbled something, sat down weakly behind my

desk. I wanted to laugh at the way fate had strangely reversed our positions. If I chose, I could cancel our order with that company and virtually destroy the man's career.

"William had been studying me. 'I know this will probably sound like a standard salesman's line'—he grinned —'but don't I know you from somewhere?' "

That night over dinner Diana refreshed William's memory. When she confronted him with the memory of his desertion, he seemed contrite, anxious to make some kind of reparation for a misdeed long done. Diana is convinced that she has been reunited with William in order that he might work out his karma and pay his debt for deserting her in another life. Diana has the memory of a recurring dream to fortify her conviction. I am not so certain that William remembers that past life, or if he is a clever opportunist who sees a way to make his present life a bit more interesting. And I am not at all convinced that Joseph can be taking this peculiar *ménage à trois* quite as matter-of-factly as Diana maintains. It is my impression that, rather than mending William's karma, Diana is going to be breaking her marriage with Joseph.

A young assistant producer told me a much more convincing story of her rediscovery of a past love, as I waited to appear on a television talk show not long ago. She had gone to a stable to spend an afternoon horseback riding when she met a teen-age boy with whom she had an instant rapport.

"I looked at him and called him Wesley, and he looked at me and called me Lillian. Neither of those names were our present ones, but they seemed to fit," she told me.

The two became good friends—only friends, she was quick to assure me—for "Wesley" was considerably younger than she. Each of them, however, felt strangely drawn to the other, and they became convinced that they had known each other in another life.

The psychic denouement came when "Lillian" dreamed

that she was being threatened by an angry man. "It was too vivid to be only a dream," she maintained. "I can remember being dressed in a style that I associate with late-frontier America. I got a name, a town in South Dakota, a state I have never visited in this life. I got a rush of apple orchards, a rural main street, parents, friends, and that furious man before me, my husband. He had found out about Wesley and me. In his rage, he threw an oil lamp at me. I screamed as the flames exploded onto my long skirt and crinolines. I was in terrible pain. Then I felt nothing, but I could see Wesley arriving too late to save me. I could see him trying to get to my room, but the flames had spread now, and he could not even climb the stairs. He stood there screaming my name.

"I watched him as he got his rifle from his saddle, sought out my husband, and shot him in the stomach. I was above everything watching, watching. I saw the funeral service that they held for my husband and for what little they could find that might be my remains. I also saw Wesley being hanged for the murder of my husband. My last emotion was feeling sorrow that my spirit could not join that of Wesley's when the rope jerked out his life."

At the same time that "Lillian" had been in the throes of her dream of remembrance, "Wesley" had to be awakened by his parents as he threshed about in the grip of a dreadful nightmare. Once they had managed to calm him, they told him that he had been screaming about a fire and how he must save Lillian.

"When we compared our dreams," the producer told me, "we found that we had both experienced a vivid recall of the life when we had been lovers. As we talked, we remembered other details, names, places, dates. I hope someday that I'll be able to travel to that town, which is now a city, and see how many things I can verify."

In an account submitted to *Fate* magazine's "My Proof of Survival" department for their August, 1969, number,

Arthur T. Huekendorff writes of an unusual occurrence which he witnessed when he was living in Shanghai in the 1920's as chairman of the board of the British-American Tobacco Company.

Yao Yu Tien, Huekendorff's close friend and business associate, had been left widowed and childless. Shortly after his wife's death, Yao told Huekendorff that a soothsayer had informed him that if he wanted many sons, he must marry a woman who was close to the earth. The seer gave Yao explicit instructions, and the businessman returned to Shanghai with a healthy eighteen-year-old bride who was already several months pregnant.

A few years later, after Yao's wife had presented him with two sons, the man confided to Huekendorff that his young wife had a most puzzling habit. On the average of one night a month, she would lie in bed and talk in a foreign tongue. Huekendorff's curiosity was aroused by his friend's report, and he asked Yao to call him next time the incident occurred.

No more than a couple of weeks passed when Yao called one night about 11:00 P.M. The young wife lay on the bed with her eyes open, but apparently unconscious of the presence of either Yao or Huekendorff. "She was silent," reads Huekendorff's account, "but after about fifteen minutes she burst into peals of laughter and then began to talk in French. My knowledge of French was not sufficient to enable me to understand what she was saying, especially as she was speaking very rapidly with all the mannerisms of a Frenchwoman, and in a voice quite unlike her own."

Huekendorff discussed the phenomenon with Dr. Fresson, his personal physician and a Frenchman. On the next occasion of the woman's weird "speaking in tongues," both Huekendorff and Dr. Fresson were in attendance.

This time the young woman's eyes were closed and she seemed unhappy. Tears streamed down her cheeks, and her speech was interrupted by violent bursts of sobbing. Dr. Fresson acknowledged that she was speaking in

French, but he said that she was using many words that had passed out of contemporary usage. Her discourse had to do with the death and funeral service of a male friend or relative who was very dear to her. "My father will not survive this," she said repeatedly.

"She continued to talk for about half an hour, asking and replying to questions," Huekendorff concludes. When the young woman finally turned over on her side and fell into a deep sleep, Dr. Fresson found that her pulse was very slow. "A discarnate spirit returned, or moments from another life?" the narrator asks.

Huekendorff's question is one which every serious researcher asks himself as he makes a study of reincarnation. Are those stories which come from the lips of entranced subjects, regardless of how convincing they may be, really memories of past lives, or may a discarnate spirit be temporarily borrowing a voice box to tell his own story? Either phenomenon is remarkable, of course, but all that appears to be the recall of past lives may not really be reincarnation. Both phenomena do, however, seem to offer validation of the personality's ability to survive the death experience.

Recently a woman came up to me after one of my lectures and said that she suspected that her son was the reincarnation of a former lover, who had been killed in Korea. "Before he left me, he said that he would return. Even if he should be killed, he said he would come back to me," she told me. According to the woman, her son strongly resembled her deceased boyfriend, both in physical appearance and in disposition. The child was born three years after the man's death overseas.

I certainly have no easy answers to dispense to individuals who throw an enigma like that at me after a lecture. Could it really be a true instance of reincarnation? Or could the woman, dissatisfied with life as a mother and housewife, recall with great affection and yearning her deceased lover and in some unconscious manner be shaping her son to resemble the ghost lover of her memory more than his physical father?

Then there is the go-go dancer in the Indiana nightclub who swears that she is a reincarnation of an ancient temple love goddess. According to the pretty and shapely young woman, she was abused terribly by a high priest, who lowered her position to that of a temple prostitute. A group of drunken men seized her one night at her alcove in the temple and demanded that she surrender her body to them in accordance with her oath of love. They violated her body so roughly and so viciously that she developed an infection from internal injuries and died.

"I know that the high priest has also been reincarnated at this time," the attractive blond says grimly. "I am seeking him out to kill him."

How will she know him?

"By his eyes. The eyes are the windows of the soul, and they never change."

And how will she kill him?

"The same way I was killed by those men when the high priest lowered my status in the temple. I will kill him with my body. I will love him to death!"

It is hard to say whether the young woman is actually convinced of her former life and her grim mission in the present, but in spite of medical assurances that one cannot die from too much lovemaking, the edge in her voice is enough to make all but the most foolhardy of men shelter his eyes when he speaks to her.